William S. Graham and Maykayla Scott

William S. Graham
Maykayla Scott

A Guide To Understanding Your Mate, And Yourself A Little Bit Better

Earthly Stories with a Heavenly Meaning

William S. Graham and Maykayla Scott

A Guide To Understanding Your Mate, And Yourself A Little Bit Better
William S. Graham and Maykayla Scott

Published By Parables
September, 2018

All Rights Reserved. No part of this book may be reproduced or utilized in any form or by any means, electronic or mechanical, including photocopying, recording, or by any information storage and retrieval system, without permission in writing from the author.

    ISBN 978-1-951497-07-1
    Printed in the United States of America

Readers should be aware that Internet Web sites offered as citations and/or sources for further information may have been changed or disappeared between the time this was written and the time it is read.

William S. Graham
Maykayla Scott

A Guide To Understanding Your Mate, And Yourself A Little Bit Better

PUBLISHED by PARABLES
Earthly Stones with a Heavenly Meaning

William S. Graham and Maykayla Scott

A Guide To Understanding Your Mate, And Yourself A Little Bit Better

Introduction

With all the knowledge we have on relationships, Maykayla Scott and I found it quite amazing if we were to write a guide about emotions, feelings, ideas, and certain things that shape and form a bond. Speaking of how bonds are formed, I have a very unique back story for you guys. Maykayla and I met 4 months ago in prison. The funny part is our prisons were only about 80 feet away from one another, which is very rare. The moment we met it was like we knew each other for many years. It's no mystery to discover Maykayla battled many relationship problems herself, which lead to a lifetime of poor choices. I myself was a very challenging young man who depicted love as a useless emotion from a relationship point of view. Regardless of our two different roles in the big bad world of prison also known as high school, we developed a very close bond with one another. As a young child I never quite understood the significance behind giving someone you love a diamond to honor the bond. I use to see personal relationships from a systemic judgmental point of view only. What I mean by having systemic judgments is we all find ourselves faced with the peer pressure of wanting to fit in with the crowd. Peer pressure as we know it has a very unique way of affecting the minds of individuals who search for acceptance. Maykayla didn't feel the need to fit in with the **in -crowd people** like I did. She was what

I called an independent young woman before it became a big popular thing in the media. Truthfully, I grew to admire her for having the courage to be her own person. As our lives would emerge from different directions, I recall sitting in a state penitentiary at the strapping age of 34 years old questioning the deeper aspects of true love. As Maykayla and I begin discussing all the things that had happened to us in our earlier relationships, we discovered a pattern between the two of us about trusting others and growing to understand true love. Then out of no where I had a bright idea, I asked Maykayla if she wanted to write a book together about the parables of love, life, and diamond –like bonds. At first she laughed at me like I had cake on my face, then she agreed to accompany me on this journey of collective thoughts. Strange as it may seem Maykayla and I both have strong desires to help others with their relationships. It's almost like we feel we have a civil duty to other people in relationships, hoping to help them or simply share our experiences with them. I believe all humans share this personal sense of conveying information with others; it is our form of communicating and connecting. One of the first lessons I learned in life was how realistic love had the power to be. Love is a very realistic entity as you may have grown to know by now. A diamond bond is a bond you can honestly look at and say "those two people belong together because they have endured the struggles of life and love together." It's evident if we were to go around and ask people how they truly feel about their bond; I'm guessing not many would admit their failing in their relationships. I'm sure you would agree admitting that you're failing or have already failed in your relationship is a very difficult thing to do. Why do you think going through a divorce is so hard for couples to do? No matter who you are, no one likes to admit they failed at love. But also if we hate failing so badly or should I say performing poorly when it comes to love, we must be willing to see many perspectives to enlighten our hearts. I ask you to journey with us as we enter a world of distant goodbyes, broken heartedness, rediscovery, understanding how to bond with your significant other creatively, relearning how to be best friends again, and a few plot twist you didn't see coming in this collection of love. Truly, we thank you for your support and great advice. We also promote you to fill out the questions in this guide and share it with your significant other- we definitely shared ours with one another. Ask yourself what kind of relationship do you have with your significant other?

William S. Graham and Maykayla Scott

A Guide To Understanding Your Mate, And Yourself A Little Bit Better

Table of Contents:

Consider What Life Has In Store For You And Your Heart

Chapter One: Pure

Chapter Two: Perfection

Chapter Three: Personality

Chapter Four: Painless

Chapter Five: Praise

Chapter Six: Purpose

Chapter Seven: Precious

Chapter Eight: Protection

Chapter Nine: Property

Chapter Ten: Peace

William S. Graham and Maykayla Scott

A Guide To Understanding Your Mate, And Yourself A Little Bit Better

Acknowledgements

First I would like to give a warm thank you to my brother Ronald Frye and sister Suzanne Gomez, who embody what it means to have a beautiful love book story relationship. Special thanks to Patricia Riley, my dear friend and beloved family member who supports all my crazy dreams. Special thanks to Nicholas Pacheco and Kelly Bruce who gave me a heart to remember and two divine faces to admire. Christopher Miller and Desiree Miller, who gave insight to the challenging world of true love and understanding life. Warm greetings to my mother Marilyn Boykin Frye, who has a heart of gold and reminds me to always use my mind every chance I get. A brotherly embrace goes out to Christopher Taylor, a dear friend and family member beyond words. Thank you to Damon Davis, my brother, who has earned the birth right of king in my book. Special warm hearted thanks to Louis Lopez and his beloved mother, Gina Lopez who have supported me and wrapped their arms around my heart. I would like to thank my dear brother, Everett Michael Harrington, who inspires me to seek better and give light to a dark situation. Special thanks to my older brother, Ceasar T. Graham, who showed me how to write my first love letter to a girl. Special thanks to Lindsay Velez and Colorado Justice Advocacy Network for showing me how beautiful hearts have a way of creating love. Special thanks to Gospel Home for Women for all their positive attributes and defining love. Special thanks to my With(in) podcast coworkers/friends: Dr. Ashley Hamilton, Andrew Draper, Denise Presson, Terry W. Mosley Jr. Chuck Martinez, Sara Berry, Michael J. Clifton, Angel Lopez, Caroline Sheahan, Julie Rada (MFA), Dr Elizabeth Catchings and my beloved pastor John Dee Jeffries , who shows me how God's love has a purpose for us all. I would like to give a special thank you to my S.U.R.G.E teammates and Rory Aktins, for supporting me through times of war and true change. I would like to give a special thanks to CDOC Director Dean Williams and God Behind Bars, Thank you to all the staff @D.R.D.C and D.W.C.F in Denver, CO and the nursing staff at both facilities. A very heart felt thank you to Maykayla's son, Jeviah, and my son Cyprese Lee Graham, for giving us both a sense of purpose and legacy to cherish dearly. Thank you all.

A Guide To Understanding Your Mate, And Yourself A Little Bit Better

Chapter One: Pure

Communication

It's no mystery, most people communicate poorly. I was one of these people who felt as if my words were lost in translation. Like many others, I knew what I wanted to say, but couldn't formulate the proper words to get my point across. As a result of my lack of communication, a lot of my relationships suffered a costly end. Like for ex: I was raised to never show emotions or display feelings to others. My entire life all my male care-givers were what many might call "men's men", who rarely showed affection to anyone, including me. I remember working for my uncle, who was a brick mason. One day while working a job with him, I cut my hand. Actually the shovel I was holding broke under the weight of the concrete, which caused a gash in my hand. It wasn't bad enough to go to the hospital, but it had a pretty good sting to it. My uncle poured rubbing alcohol over my hand, and I made a wincing face to show how the pain was affecting me. Would you believe my uncle looked at me like I was a Burmese cat or something? Then he belted in an amusing chuckle, as if to say "that's not pain boy!"

I say all this to highlight how communication grew an ugly plant in my back yard. Showing affection became difficult for me as life would continue. I even spent many years judging others who were overly affectionate. People who showed affection to me were classified as soft or, over sensitive. When the truth was I was quite jealous of individuals who had the ability to express themselves in many different forms. I wanted so badly to be one of them, a person who told others how I felt deep down inside. I told myself I could change, but I didn't know how to change. In this day and age, we are granted the pleasure to raise our kids without mental setbacks. (Some of us, not all of us agree with this new profound way of raising our kids) I am hopeful to understand how certain mental blocks are being removed from the next generation to come. This in return, allows the ongoing growth of all who see, believe, and adapt to the daily inserts. Communication is one of the most important elements to any relationship, especially if the bond serves as a potential diamond bond. The power of communication is like water and air in your relationship, definitely necessities in our daily lives. It is a proven fact most failed relationships are traced back to a lack of communication. And the main question most couples ask themselves is how do I find the right time to talk to my significant other?

I once heard someone say "perfect timing is like coordinating your daily outfits."

Amazingly to discover how many people, who stare at their closet, confused?

Picking the perfect time to talk to your mate takes more skills than you would imagine.

A Guide To Understanding Your Mate, And Yourself A Little Bit Better

Here are a few examples when not to talk to your mate about important issues. When they roll over in the morning, mouth smelling like a dragon's fart, with more eye boogers than the law should allow- that is not a good time. When the playoffs are in full affect, with 3 seconds left on the clock- that is not a good time. When the family comes over for Thanksgiving dinner, and everyone is running around like they have no sense- that is not a good time. When your mate has a crying baby in their arms that is not a good time to have a deep conversation. You may feel it is the perfect time to talk about whatever is on your mind, but it is not. Say if your mate has a difficult time handling stress and retaining the information you are trying to relay to them. Nothing you say will reach them if they've built a defensive wall around them. It's not personal, just how we are wired as humans. Learning to access your mate's situation is very important toward your maturity levels. This is important because it grants you the ability to view yourself inside the relationship and outside the relationship. I was talking to this guy one time about his ex-girlfriend, who despite many years of tolerance, decided it would be best if they went their separate ways. The guy explained to me how the relationship suffered from a lack of understanding and communication daily. What do you know about cause and effect?

(Cause equals Effect)
As we know, if we do something, we should expect something to come from it. It's that simple. You steal a piece of candy or a car; you can expect a hardship to accompany that action. Especially when the action has no rightful cause to support its justification. This way of

cause and effect works the same way in relationships. If you cheat on your mate, then you cheat yourself out of earning their full trust. If you lie to your mate, you are lying to yourself as well. I can't tell you how many people I talk too about their trust issues with their mates. You should see their faces when I tell them it's their fault for the mistrust in their relationship. Their eyes get as big as flying saucers when they discover the mistrust was a joint effort. The cause and effect of mistrust in every relationship starts with the lack of communication. If you and your mate don't speak about tough issues, the mistrust builds up inside.

Over the years I discovered how the effects of mistrust and the lack of communication caused me a lot of hurt and harm. No matter how many mates tried to get me to open up, the results were pretty much the same. What are you struggling with on a daily basis? Describe the way you feel when you are struggling with these daily emotions? How are you overcoming these emotions?

Ask your mate if there's anything that stands out in your relationship you two might need to work on?

_____
_____
_____
_____
_____

Dissatisfaction

A Guide To Understanding Your Mate, And Yourself A Little Bit Better

You know how when you have a craving for something like chocolate or potato chips, you go on the prowl for these things. When you finally taste what you've been craving this whole time, is it as enjoyable as you imagined? Yes. No.

I believe we call that dissatisfaction or satisfaction- which also reflects to our daily relationships. In our daily relationships we see the initial craving for a mate which gradually advances to attaining thus said craving. Meaning we'll do almost anything to get what we are craving. We tell our inner selves, we must have it, and nothing else will suffice. We don't allow nothing to stop us on our mission or persecute to satisfaction. In this lies a problem for some, seeing how we all are different with our own feelings, emotions, and satisfaction measurements. To put it plainly, some people only crave you for the moment- the right now. They're captivated by their instant urges which disappear the moment you give them what they want. Just like the wandering traveler who eats at everyone's house, drinks their nectar, and has a grand laugh for the ages- then hits the road. You can't take it personal, because you're the one who let them into your home or should I say your heart. It doesn't matter how intoxicating the weary traveler's stories may be to you, it's best to sustain yourself for their departure. Most of us try our hardest to hold on to what we feel will free us, when that's not the case at all. To be truly happy in life, inner peace must play a very vital role in one's soul. The soul of every being searches for inner peace during an entire lifetime. Satisfaction has a lot to do with the inner peace within one's own heart before it is embraced as a couple. Inner peace for some may be cooking, writing, playing sports, music, cleaning, and drawing, building things with your hands, and anything that brings the heart true joy. I always say I write to rejuvenate my soul and open my eyes to other perspectives. We must grow to understand, it is not what we hold on to which free us, but the things we let go of that empowers us. At times we search for satisfaction in others to make ourselves happy, unaware happiness resides in the heart. Like many others, I've heard this saying more times than I can count, but no matter how many times I've heard it- the truth is still the truth. The truth is if you're unhappy, nothing outside of yourself, will bring you joy. I've heard it said "the road to a beautiful life starts with a smile." The moment I learned how to be happy inside my heart, I could careless about other people's opinions. I found myself satisfied with my own happiness for once in my lifetime.

A Guide To Understanding Your Mate, And Yourself A Little Bit Better

Chapter Two: Perfection

First let's be honest by stating what's in our hearts, a lot of us have trust issues with our significant others. As you sit there reading this, whole heartedly, you understand how important trust is in any relationship. Having a strong sense of trust between you and your significant other is something you have to establish like a foundation. By establishing this proper foundation in your relationship, you are granted the opportunity to build levels of maturity in your relationship. Let's say your significant other and you are struggling with your daily trust issues, it's becoming a constant problem. You feel your mate constantly lies to you about frivolous things. Your mate believes you are always cheating on them, and mistreating them. Clearly the state of trust in this relationship sucks and needs a dashing make over. In this scenario, the foundations in which the grounds of trust have been established are shaky. The mistrust comes into play when one mate discovers the other mate is against them instead of being with them. This happens when certain things are revealed to each other which paint your significant other in an unexpected light. Here's the thing about expectations, people are complicated and quite confused at times about each other's interpretations and expectations. What this means is we as couples or significant others don't always take the proper time to examine one another. Here are a few questions for you to ask yourself during your own private time.

The Trust Test

1. How well do I really know my significant other? Be sure to contemplate the other sides of your mate you haven't seen yet. Most couples call this the ugly side of love.

_____

_____

2. Am I able to trust my mate with my life and my heart? Is there anything in the past which would make you second guess this question?

_____

_____

3. Do you believe your mate is cheating on you behind your back? What evidence have you discovered which gives you merit on this issue?

_____

_____

4.
5. **Lastly how would you say your mate sees you, which may or may not have altered your bond?**
6. _____

_____

These questions are very important as we begin to build the foundations of trust in our relationships. For example: let's say you were at a shopping mall and some random store caught your eye. You walk in the store with hope hopes of checking it out. Upon your investigation you discover this store is the worst store you've ever attended. Would you go back to this store over and over again? Of course not right! You were mistreated and felt unappreciated in that particular store, this is how you felt.

And as humans this is how we catalog bad experiences in our minds. Unfortunately places of businesses and relationships are two different entities altogether. The difference between relationships and places of businesses, simply resides in one factor, expectations, and how we perceive things. A healthy relationship requires proper skills and certain levels of growth to establish a solid foundation. Once trust has been established in the relationship, each party feels they have an equal stake in the foundation. This allows both parties to begin building the bond together, instead of individually. A dear friend of mine, Damon L. Davis, once told me "the moment you trust yourself, everyone follows suit."

Growing up I can honestly say I struggled with trusting others. The word "trust" to me was a foreign word people threw around loosely. The strange part is I trusted team mates who I played sports with throughout my young adulthood. It took me a couple years to admit I didn't trust young women particularly. I mean I was infatuated with young women, but I didn't trust them at all. If you were to ask me what exactly fuelled this lack of trust I would say the abandonment issues I had with my mother. My mother was sent to prison to serve a 20 year sentence during my childhood. I recall holding a grudge against her for the abandonment I felt. I believe this sense of abandonment caused me to reject and distrust young women growing up, plus I was very mean spirited in my heart. The moment I found myself in prison after 7 years I grew to truly appreciate the essence of women. The revelation in my heart became a lesson of ages, saying you have to learn to trust yourself before you can trust anyone else.

Would you say trust is earned in your heart or automatically given?

_____
_____
_____

Why or why not?

_____
_____
_____
_____
_____
_____

Here is a quote from a very dear friend of mine "If your eyes and heart are open, you can see and feel trust in those around you" Terry W. Mosley Jr.

When my dear friend Terry W. Mosley Jr. shared this collection of words with me I was enlightened and forced to ask myself what have I denied my heart in the past? I asked myself did I deny my heart the discovering of love in the past, confused why I couldn't find it every time I searched for its essence. I believe we all tend to forget how personal love is to the soul. I would like to thank Terry for giving me the gift of thought, and for challenging my perspective on sight.

Flavor

As we look at the essence of a healthy relationship, I present you with a metaphor of thought. Let's say your relationship is a giant pot that you can cook anything you want inside. Everything you put in this pot makes up the perfect relationship (which truly does not exist) but we'll pretend it does. As you look at your bare pot, what are some of the ingredients you feel are needed to create a healthy relationship?

For example: someone might say I require creating more passion in my relationship. Then you would put passion in the pot, mixing it with everything you already attained. After you create a healthy relationship by putting the proper ingredients in it, ask yourself how does it taste? Remember it has to taste good toward you and your mates likings. If it doesn't taste good, what's the point right? My advice to you would be, add a little spice and sugar sometimes, trust me it won't kill you.

Maykayla, what are some things you would say adds flavor to any healthy relationship?

I believe these things add favor to all relationships; trust, love, understanding, ideas, support, care, patience, struggle, hard work, honor, forgiveness, time, passion, humor, strength, and courage.

Confidence

What is it about the person who walks in the room full of confidence which makes us second guess ourselves? Is it safe to say people who have overly self-confidence are full of themselves, or are we suffering from low self- esteem? If I were to ask you to rate your confidence level as a single person compared to how you feel when you're in a relationship, where would you score?

<u>Single</u>

.Very low
. Low
. Moderate
. Above average
. Very high

<u>In a Relationship</u>

. Very low
. Low
. Moderate
. Above average
. Very high

Clearly it is no mystery to discover how important self-assurance becomes in any relationship, yet alone our intimate bonds. How about this for an example, have you ever been in a room full of people, and felt underdressed? You look around to see if anyone is underdressed like yourself. Wishing someone sent you a text about what to wear. Self- confidence works the same way in our daily relationships. We build self confidence in one another by spending time with one another. By spending time with one another, the confidence level builds together, instead of separately. When you engage in a relationship with your significant other you must understand the energy levels between the two of you. Good energy raises the levels of confidence in your relationship. Bad energy brings these levels of self-confidence down. Like for example, yelling at each other causes low self-esteem and creates doubt in your relationship. This created level of doubt has the power to ruin your relationship and destroy your self-confidence.

Change

Describe the things about me you would change or improve if you could?

_____
_____
_____

Why would you change these things about me? And how would these changes improve our relationship?

_____
_____
_____
_____
_____

Amazingly, we find ourselves deeply contemplating these questions in our hearts. I believe every significant other would say "I wouldn't change a single thing about you", as if the pretense of your alteration has to be negative. The alteration in your significant other could be you wish they could see how talented they are. Or maybe you would change your mate's drinking habits which have become a hindrance in your relationship. Most often than most when people look at themselves they quickly highlight their good qualities, and submerge their bad attributes. Some psychologist would call this the two way mirror syndrome. The two way mirror syndrome occurs when actions are displayed, unaware of how others perceive these same actions. For example let's say your significant other has a drinking problem that affects the relationship and their well being. It is best for the relationship if you are supportive during the seeking of a positive solution. It has been proven that if a significant other is supportive of another mate it will cause the bond to grow closer in fact.

Chapter Three: Personality

Replica

You know what I learned about myself a few years into my journey? I learned I didn't know how to acknowledge my type or preference of woman. At first I didn't know I had a type, and secondly I didn't how to cherish the type I did like. Crazy right! I even remember telling my childhood friends how bored I use to get with the young women I would choose. I discovered it wasn't the fact I was bored, more less the fact I was choosing young women who did not peek my interest. Saying that brings me to the realization of how for a long time I chose replicas of the women who did not peek my interest, wondering why my relationships did not work out. As I begin to realize the error of my ways, I quickly tried to change what had become a habit of mine. This is what I like to call **the quick sand** stage. The quick sand stage is where I found myself stuck in the same state of choice when it came to picking what I truly desired in a woman. To put it in better terms, choosing the proper mate is like looking at a giant menu and having to make a choice. During my journey of discovering myself, I found I preferred women who presented a challenge. I discovered I desired women who were strong willed and open to over coming odds. Why? I preferred women who were strong willed because I related better to their struggle. I felt their struggle to intertwine with my goals to be better and achieve higher understanding. At first I spent many years dodging strong willed women because I knew they wouldn't put up with my nonsense, and I wasn't ready to grow up. I know refusing to choose a certain type of woman because they wouldn't allow me to play my childish silly games might sound pretty sick, but at least I'm being honest. As I referenced in one of my other books called "Hurt People…Hurt People" the moment I felt unwanted by my parents I projected those feelings on to everyone else. Those projected feelings toward my parents created a sense of low self-esteem in my heart. These same feelings caused neglect and a level of hurt I transferred to others, especially young women.

Are you stuck on your ex?

_____

_____

What is it about your ex you desire so much?

_____

_____

Do you find yourself choosing replicas of the same mate?

_____

_____

Explain to yourself why you prefer this type of person in your life?

_____
_____

What about you do you notice gets sacrificed once you're in a relationship?

_____
_____

First Impressions

      The first time you met your significant other, what kind of impression did you make on them? Were you smooth when you and your significant other met for the first time, or were you on the dance floor with your shirt pulled over your head? First impressions are very vital when meeting someone; especially the people we are destine to spend the rest of our lives with. First impressions give us a sense of control, like a choice we don't know we have until we make that choice. The most interesting thing about first impressions is you never know how someone feels about what you're doing because it's their perspective of you. What I mean by this is you could feel you did everything wrong on a date, and you might have made a complete fool of yourself, but this doesn't change how your significant other viewed you. That's why they say "the power of first impressions create a lasting affect on the heart." Remember the movie "Hitch" starring Will Smith, where he explained how when someone first meets someone else, the connection of thought has a way of working itself out for the better. First impressions work the same way as we grow to understand what we perceive to be true is not what attracts us. For example: let's say you and your significant other met on the dance floor of a late night club. Let's say you only had a couple of drinks, but your significant other was completely hammered as the two of you danced the night away. Most people would say being drunk when you meet your mate is something to be frowned upon, but there is no right answer or wrong answer when it comes to first impressions. I remember I took this young lady out to the movies one day. The moment we arrived at the movie theater everything seem to go completely wrong, as I tried to be cool. The first thing that occurred was I forgot to open the door for her as we entered the door. The young lady was more than vocal about my conduct, and it made the date a disaster in my eyes. After the date was coming to an end I drove the young lady home, and formally apologized to her. The young lady informed me she had a lovely time out with me. I was completely shocked to discover I had done everything right on the date. My dear friend Christopher Miller told me something very profound I'll never forget. He told me "everyone is watching each other for the first time like movies, some of these movies are sad and end poorly and some of these movies end victoriously."

As Christopher Miller told me this I asked myself if my life was a movie what title would I name my movie. The name of my life movie would be called "A Grade Unlearned"

A Guide To Understanding Your Mate, And Yourself A Little Bit Better

Die for You

I lay there
Beside your heart
Like a piece of art
Forgive me if I stare
Forgive if I care
Addicted to the future
Life is unfair
Like a pair of shoes
We step out with pride
Laughing, but dying inside
As if we have to hide our feelings
Burnt alive
Screaming for love to save us
As if Superman had an off day
No one to trust
But you
Do you know what that feels like?
To hold on to love for dear life
As if the price was too high to bear
So I sit there
At the check out line alone
Asking where?
Where is love?

William S. Graham and Maykayla Scott

Annoying Habits

I can't tell you how many times I've heard couples say their annoying habits presented a challenge in their relationship. I believe every couple would agree the annoying habits they have formulates the bond over time. If I had to describe how or why this occurs, I would just simply say people get use to each other's habits. Let's say for instance your significant other has a nasty habit of chewing with their mouth open. Let's say you can over look this annoying habit when the two of you are eating dinner at home, but what happens when you go out? Are you embarrassed by the certain looks smeared on your friend's faces? I'm pretty sure the average person would be quite embarrassed about this annoying habit. How would you present this information to your significant other?

_____

_____

Would you let them know their annoying habits embarrassed you to the point of shame?

_____

_____

Would you yell at them and scorn them like a child?

_____

_____

I know this might sound quite minutia to some, but to others I'm guessing this issue holds a lot of weight in their relationship. I believe if we look at the annoying habits from a more serious perspective, it'll change how we view these habits. For instance let's say your significant other has an annoying habit of cheating on you. I'm sure you would agree having someone cheat on you compared to leaving the toilet seat up are two different things. How about this example, your significant other has an annoying habit like hiding money all over the house. Every time you look inside a vase or knock over a shoe box, you find stashes of money. Now this could be seen as a very annoying habit from a certain perspective, but what if you lose your job? Would you agree this annoying habit of stashing money around the house after you get laid off from your job isn't such an annoying habit after all? My personal advice would be to make you spend a lot of time dating and getting to know everything about the person before you get serious. I believe it's better to date someone for awhile than rush into an early divorce.

The Playoffs

There's only five seconds left on the clock when your favorite player shoots the game winning shot. As you hold your breath with the back of your eye balls refusing to blink, suddenly the television goes completely black. You turn around to see your significant other holding the remote with a look that says **yeah I did it**. Then you hear the words most people fear, "we have to talk." As you hear your significant other say these words to you, a part of you desires to run out of the house and never come back. The other part of you sits emotionless as if someone poured ice water down your shirt. That would suck! The truth is you've probably neglected the levels of communication well needed between you and your significant other. By you failing to properly communicate with your significant other, now you've missed the last precious moments of a playoff game you really wanted to see. I would advise you to have any important conversation with your significant other before football season begins. And look at it like this, losing the game hurts your heart but losing your significant other hurts your house hold.

Numbers 7: 12-18

You're Right…I'm Wrong…I'm Sorry

I'm willing to bet 20 million dollars, which I don't have by the way, somewhere in the world a lot of women just took a large deep breath. Yes ladies your eyes do not deceive you in the least, a man just wrote the words you're right…I'm wrong…I'm sorry. Guys of the world, believe it or not that's all women want to hear from men. I believe us as men spend so much time trying to explain ourselves or justify our actions to women, we don't realize they do not want to hear it. I learned a long time ago that trying to have a successful argument with women is a losing battle beyond words. I can hear the guys of the world right now saying "why you telling them that!" "You're a sell out brother!" they say. "I'm not reading this crap!" Well guys of the world here's my counter offer to your comments and unrealistic mumbling. First and foremost, anyone who knows women or has a mother would tell you the truth. You can't argue with a woman, no matter how good you are at talking. Secondly why would you waste your time trying to prove to her that you're right and she's wrong- think about it from another perspective buddy? Lastly if your end results are to be sleeping on the couch just to be right, you're an idiot. I'll rather be wrong in a warm bed beside her, than right on the couch all by myself. Think about it for a minute, then repeat after me you're right…I'm wrong…I'm sorry. I would say sometimes winning an argument over your significant other isn't always worth losing their respect.

William S. Graham and Maykayla Scott

Chapter Four: Painless

Can't Raise a Man

I remember the first time I heard the song "Can't Raise a Man" by K. Michelle, I was scratching my head. As I listened to the contents of the song I couldn't help but connect to the lyrics. The song depicts an independent woman who is in love with a man boy struggling to grow up. The movie "Baby Boy" directed by John Singleton does a great job of painting a clear picture of a young black male forced to mature and be a man. Maykayla and I begin this conversation by stating the problem with most young men trapped in the urban youth find themselves perpetuating the cycle of poor fatherhood and failing to realize the elements of true love. (I was guilty of this same crime) I remember this elderly lady telling me something profound when I was fairly young. She said "babies are having babies nowadays!" I didn't quite understand what she was saying back then, but now I comprehend her entire message from a personal perspective. Maykayla and I agreed on a few things during our discussions of what it takes to grow up. Maykayla wrote me saying "I'm done with fixer upper men!" I had an idea what she was hinting at, but I wanted to hear her expound on the subject more, so I asked her to explain what she meant. She was very narrative about her expression on the subject of being finished with men who acted like children. "Do you know what it feels like to have your heart broken by someone you completely trusted with your life?" she wrote boldly. I sat there emotionless while reading her words of pain, thinking of all the women I hurt in my early lifetime. But I wrote her back a few days later saying "No I don't know what it feels like to have my heart broken by a significant other I loved and trusted with all my heart." I remember writing these solid words; I've never really loved any young lady whole heartedly." I wrote to her "I can't begin to compare my struggles to the many sacrifices you've endured with your past heartaches and snares, but I do know what it feels like to love someone who didn't love me back." I wrote "If you had to pin point where you went wrong, where would you start?" Maykayla answered this question by saying "where I believe I went wrong was trying to fix the ghost of my past." What she was referring to was she spent a countless amount of time trying to help men who were completely helpless. As she used the word (ghost) to describe the men of her past, I couldn't help but realize how innocent we both were when it came to love. Then my mind started entertaining how many men had broken her heart and did it start with her father. I wrote to her I wasn't truly proud of my past actions, how I treated young women. She informed me I was young at the time, and said we all do things as kids, and then wish we could take these things back. It felt so good to see those words on a piece of paper as if I had been waiting on those exact words for what felt like a lifetime. I couldn't wait to explain to her my stages of growth into manhood. And just to give you a sense of

A Guide To Understanding Your Mate, And Yourself A Little Bit Better

shock, as these words embrace paper I sat in a 6x9 prison cell in a Colorado state prison. I've been incarcerated since the early age of 18 years old; I'm 35 years old now. I haven't seen or spoken to none of my family members since I was 16 years old. In 2004 I was sentence to 72 years for aggravated robbery, which I whole heartedly regret. And yes, I'm sure by now you've made up your mind who's the beauty and who's the beast in this little fairy tale of ours. But before you completely throw me to the gallows please know I traveled the long way home to become the man I am today. Since my incarceration I've graduated over 27 cognitive classes, including attaining my G.E.D and 7 Habits of Highly Effective People. I'm certified clinical aid nurse and hospice care worker- taking care of the sick and dying offenders in my current prison for 4 years now. I have been a volunteer peer mentor for the pass 4 years as well. I trained under Damon L. Davis and Alex Manigo who serve as peer mentor leaders in the daily orientation of every offender sentenced to the CDOC (Colorado Department of Corrections). I am also a published author 5 times over. The names of my books available on Amazon, Barnes & Noble, and Google Play are "Leave the Door Open", "Hurt People...Hurt People", "40 Degrees of Love", "and 50 Degrees of Love", and "The Locksmith of Love". I have two more books due to be released in the early year of 2020, entitled "Get Off the Tricycle" and "Love Is Coated With Honey". I am a group leader of the Denver Complex for DU PAI (Denver University Prison Arts Initiative). I also serve as the resident poet and creative consultant on a prison pod cast entitled "With (In)", where we are shifting the conversation on who is in prison? This beautiful project is supported by DU PAI and our beloved founder Dr. Ashley Hamilton, the facilities of Sterling Correctional facility and the Denver Complex. I am the host of a show called (Will's Corner), where I interview other artist based residents from other facilities in the state of Colorado. I also founded my own non-profit organization and greeting card Company beside my dear friend Christopher Taylor called A.L.O.T Foundation (Actually Living off Talent). I know what you're saying, not too bad for a prisoner wouldn't you agree? But don't get me wrong, I'm not a perfect man by far but I do know growing up takes a lot of strength and will power. And personally I believe a lot of pray helps us all through the struggles we endure on the daily. Like my Aunt Ann Johnson would say "there's nothing sadder than a grown ass boy who's scared to grow up and be a man."

Here's a poem I wrote a year ago entitled...

"Grow Up"

Moving fast in life
Slow up
Like congested traffic, what's wrong...what's right?
A traitor of my own ways
When time slept on the roof
And love needed proof
Just to stay
I was right there beside you
At least in my mind I was
Searching for a heart like yours
Trying to find
Sunset warmth

In my soul
I found the cold
Maturing like a wild flower
Someone left me on side of the road
Purple moons I stared at
Telling myself the future must be mine
It's funny how in God's time everything is redefined
The first design being love

Intimacy

Alright, let's say there was an intimacy class and the teacher asked the entire group of students to describe intimacy, is it safe to say a lot of us would have poor grades? I'd probably be the student leaning over Maykayla's shoulder, cheating off her homework. This basically means I'm kind of a slow learner when it comes to being intimate with others, or at least I use to be. Intimacy reminds me of speaking another language that seems difficult at first, but if you stick with it you'll reap the benefits of your hard labor. When I was fairly young I thought intimacy only had to do with sex or some form of sexual intercourse. No one informed me how powerful intimacy truly is to everyone especially those in long term relationships. Like take holding hands in public for example. Most couples view holding hands in public as a teenager attribute deemed unnecessary to adult relationships. Would you agree or disagree that holding hands in public with your significant other is necessary?

_____

_____

Why or why not?

_____

_____

How good are you at showing public affection with your significant other?

_____

_____

*Rate yourself- Poor   Average   above Average

Here's a unique story I would like to share with you guys if you bare with me. When I was a teenager I remember seeing an elderly couple holding hands in the mall one day. As I walked pass them in what seemed like slow motion, a smile appeared across my face with a hint of humor in my heart. I'll never forget seeing two elderly people holding hands without a care in the world. I must tell you seeing the elderly couple holding hands at such an elderly age reminded me of an act of defiance or non conformity. A part of me cheered the couple on as my heart questioned their journey of love. Looking back on that very rare moment I wished I had the courage to walk up to them and inquire about their lives. When I approach the topic of intimacy I'm constantly reminded of the elderly couple who defined the odds of change and challenged the elements of everlasting love. At times I find myself questioning how would I cherish one of God's creatures of beauty? For all the lovers of the world here's a passage to consider about intimacy and compassion. Imagine pouring warm water on your significant other's head, washing their hair with care. If you take your finger tips and massage their head it'll release the built up tension and relax their mind. Here's something else you can do together as a bonging agent. Gather two wash basins and fill them mid level with warm water. Pour some smell good in each water basin, but be mindful of any powders or shampoos that may cause your significant other to have an allergic reaction to any of the chemicals. Anyway while you're sitting there soaking your feet in separate wash basins, this is a perfect time for conversation. After you've finished talking to one another, not blaming, shaming, or guilt tripping one another, take a giant beach towel and dry each other's feet off. The final step is rubbing lotion on your significant other's feet, and letting them know you appreciate them for all they do for you and the family. This brings Maykayla and I to another subject ringing truth in all relationships, we call it appreciation.

Appreciation

Let's say your significant other has been working very hard, and you just want to pay homage to their essence. I have the perfect ways to show them you care dearly for their extra hard work. First you have to understand how appreciation is one of the most powerful agents in any relationship. Any couple who has been together for quite some time would agree you have to have appreciation in your relationships. Like for example, you can show gratitude to your significant other by serving them breakfast in bed. I know that might sound quite cheesy or cliché, but remember it's not about you- it's about the appreciation of someone you care about. Also you should keep in mind showing appreciation to someone doesn't always have to be a dramatic ordeal. Many people would tell you, some of the most special things people have done for them were quite simple but heart felt. Like for ex: writing a sincere letter to your significant other about anything. You can give your heart in a collection of words. How about writing your significant other a letter pertaining to all the things you're thankful for, and please don't write the letter like a 3rd grader. When composing a heart felt letter for your significant other, it's alright to spend a little time putting it together. Also showing appreciation for your significant other should always be something which resembles your style and not someone else's style. Trust me when I tell you, if you cherish your beloved mate every once in awhile it'll surely improve your relationship to the highest accord.

Love Yourself

Without question I'm pretty sure you've heard the age old saying "you have to love yourself before you can love someone else." Despite how old this saying may seem, it is true for all. But hold up one minute; let's challenge this notion to a certain degree. Is it possible to love someone more than you love yourself? Yes. I believe people love many things before they love themselves. Honesty I would say the ability to love something or someone before you love yourself is a self less act of care. Think about it like this if you may, if your relationship was a football team, would you want your team mate to love the team more than they love themselves? I know I enjoy a team mate who is willing to sacrifice body and limb for the sake of the team. Truthfully what I am saying is we all understand what it means to dedicate heart and soul to a note worthy cause, but loving our inner selves and taking care of our selves is what serves the bond the best.

Loyalty

I remember the first time I heard the word "loyalty",

I didn't know what it actually meant. I told myself I was completely aware what the word loyalty entailed, but that was a bold face lie. The funny part about my early stages of loyalty stemmed from playing sports and defending my younger brothers from being bullied. I was completely oblivious to the word loyalty being demonstrated from a relationship perspective. I know how that reads among many people, and growing up in a masochistic world where feelings, emotions, and thoughts of care for the opposite sex were quite primeval, it was normal. As shockingly as it may seem I didn't have a revelation toward my approach on loyalty and intimate relationships until much later. When I was 17 years old a young lady reformed my perspective on the definition of loyalty by relating to me on my level. She said "you pride yourself on being someone who holds loyalty very regal among your male friends, but when it comes to your female friends equality and respect falls short." I thought about what she said to me for a few days before I truly acknowledged her wisdom. Then I noticed something that was more disturbing than what she said to me. I realized I didn't have any female friends. It was evident at the time, every female outside of my immediate family members and school teachers were individuals who I had sexual intercourse with. I didn't have one female friend at that point in time of my life, and that's when I realized I was a chauvinistic young man. I told myself I needed to honestly work on my perspectives of young women, and my communicational skills. As time went by I found myself growing more advanced in my verbal skills, and I developed a new profound admiration for female companionship. I would say when I was ready to grow God sent me a couple beautiful women who I now consider my beloved friends for life, and I am forever loyal to them. The first time I heard the word loyalty I thought I knew what it meant, that was a long time ago, now I know what it truly means.

"Loyalty is a gift we give to people who are worthy of its true essence"
Everett Michael Harrington

Kids Change Everything

Despite what you might believe to be true, kids change everything in your relationship. First and foremost you can kiss private bedtime goodbye. Well completely saying goodbye **to private bedtime is such a harsh notion to accept. How about if we use some** better words to describe the unfortunate decline in your private bedtime activities. How about if we use the words going out of business soon? Does that paint a better picture for you when it comes to the kids interrupted your bedtime escapades? I figured it would. Remember a time when couples would actually plan out having kids. I know that notion seems quite ancient in this day and age but it's definitely true to know people at one point in time actually planned to have kids. Now as you may know I (William) was not one of these people who dared to plan out having kids, matter fact I was shocked where they came from in the first place. When the mother of my son (Vanessa) told me we were having a kid I was looking around like someone who didn't quite get the joke. I can honestly say I was not ready to be a father, but I can say I was elated to be a father. I wanted my child to look up to me with a sense of honor and bold legacy. Sadly to say I failed my son and the mother of my child for many years before actually getting my act together. "The worst things are done with the greatest intentions" I learned to love this quote because of how true it resonated in my life. I can say I had greatest intentions when I chose to rob people with a gun, and earn money but the truth is I was a coward at time. The truth is I wasn't ready to grow up and be a real man just yet. I, like many others, was a young boy who wanted to play house only to discover I didn't know anything about life or love. I remember telling myself as a young child, I wouldn't grow up to be like my father- who I labeled a dead beat dad for many years. I use to hold so much hate in my heart for him, and seeing how I've never met my father some would even say I hated a ghost for many of my growing years. The common fact with most young black men states how we are unprepared to live life, raise families, and have significant others. The blind truth is kids change everything in our daily lives, just when you think you have it figured out something else goes wrong. Some people would even say life is designed to throw us off our game, leaving us confused about our next steps we are destine to make. While others would say having kids and trying to properly plan for them is like studying for a test all night long, only to have the teacher change the test to something you didn't study for. When having kids the best thing you could ever do is enjoy the moments while they last, because once the trill is gone it's gone. One of my favorite songs is by country singer Darius Rucker entitled "It Won't Be Like This for Long". This song by Darius Rucker helped me put a lot of my perspectives about having kids and spending the precious moments of life together in peace.

    I'll end this piece with a quote from my dear friend Christopher Miller.

    "Life is like hearing the same joke over and over again –you might say you hate it until you go deaf"

Chapter Five: Praise

Relationship Deal Breakers

If I had to consider a solid deal breaker when it comes to terminating a relationship I would have to say anyone who neglects me or cheats on me. I can honestly say I could not be with anyone who cheated on me and If I were to engage in any kind of personal relationship with someone who cheated on me or abandoned me, I wouldn't be able to focus on anything but how they neglected me. Have you ever been with someone who did something you knew you couldn't stomach? I remember cheating on a young lady about 7 years ago, who found the strength to forgive me. Her and I talked and decided it would be best if we tried to repair the relationship. A month later, she informed me that she was unable to carry on in the relationship; we said our goodbyes and went our own separate ways. I believe that was the first time I discovered what it meant to have someone not be able to stomach my actions. I believe we are all like that, realizing how disappointment has a way of showing us what we are expecting from our significant others. Some people possess the ability to outcome feats and let downs that others couldn't stomach to save their lives, this one would describe as a stronger sense of love. I wouldn't particular call it a stronger sense of love whenever someone can forgive significant other for doing something which caused them harm. I would just classify the sense of care as a laser focus to make the bond they have with that person work. The other day Maykayla and I were sharing something with one another, and she presented me with a question for thought. She said "how do you rebuild something, relationship wise, which never had the proper time to formulate?" I thought to myself wow! By her saying this to me I was truly given something to ponder over night. After thinking about the question Maykayla presented to me something my heart already knew, it's almost impossible to rebuild what you've never had, but if it never existed then you can begin to rebuild it. What I wanted to tell her was everybody discovers love at their own time; some people go an entire life time and never discover true love. I know this to be true because I remember telling myself at a very young age, love is not real. I mean clearly I knew love was real, but what I was saying was I didn't have any faith in love. I realized how wrong I was, and I adopted a whole new concept when it came to the subject of love. I don't know about you guys, but I use to treat love like a convenient store. I use to rush into relationships, like most of us do, unaware of any dangers or who is who? Just like any other convenient store, after I got what I wanted, sadly I was gone as if I never existed in that space of time. If I had to describe my perspective in a real life form I would say I approached love like most young actors approach Hollywood, CA, (from a very gullible point of view). Like I said it didn't take long to realize how wrong I was when it came to love. Like my publisher Pastor John Dee Jeffries would say true love is found in God's love first. And I must say discovering God within my heart was the first stage of me learning how powerful love can be. Maykayla and I were both raised in the south with church- like back grounds that introduced us to the element of God. But like I always say "there's a difference between going to church, and believing in the spirit of God." Some would say it's the same thing, when the truth is there's a big difference. Even though we all feel we have deal breakers that hinder us from accepting disappointment, it is best we know the power of forgiveness is one of the hardest things to master. True love has the power to overcome all odds and refuses to yield to anything that doesn't resemble its essence. I believe love challenges us all to be our greatest selves, and honor one another through care, compassion, truth, words, and always faith.

"Some people train themselves not to feel love out of fear of losing it from their grasp, but when they get a chance to hold it again- they never let go"

Angel Lopez

History

Since the beginning of time it has been said the betrayal of a lover ranks higher than most. Indeed I would agree the betrayal of a lover ranks higher than most. But I am forced to question why I believe this to be true? On a personally note I believe this question serves as a greater sense of thought to all mankind and lovers alike. As we look throughout history we see how love has played a major role in our daily interpretations. Have you ever been hurt by someone you were in love with?

_____

How did being hurt by someone you were in love with affect you the most?

_____

When you look around are there things that remind you of that particular person everyday?

_____

Name how some of things about your ex that you liked or disliked

_____
_____

Maykayla and I know what you probably saying "I don't want to think about my ex who I call the scum of the earth." we understand why you feel that way, but we would like you try to answer these questions to help you cope with the ill feelings you might be hoarding against your ex-lover. Trust us when we tell you it helps you get over the broken emotions that never go anywhere until you face them. The history of most couples who suffer a divorce or separation seems to read out of a movie. Or maybe you witnessed your parents going through daily relationship issues that implanted a seed of doubt in your mind. As we look at life and love it is very important to understand how the affects of the past plays a vital role in our decision making process. A few years ago I wrote a poem on this subject and I would like to share it with you guys if don't mind. The poem is called "Existing"

> Falling from a place in my heart
> Unable to catch myself before the hurt
> I woke up years later
> Tasting foothills of dirt
> No broken bones
> Just a few sticks and stones, and the wrong intentions
> A gut wrenching feeling
> Walking on the ceiling
> Not to mention, you told me you were healing
> But you were not
> I asked you "what was wrong?"
> You responded "do you know how long you've been gone?"
> I didn't know-
> You did
> Many years later
> I sat there watching the tears turn into favors
> Each one breaking her face like fears
> Trying to savor the moment
> Break the soul
> Hurt the heart
> Make it cold
> Transform the ways
> Honor the days
> Collect the toll
> Forget the past
> Eat the last

Play the role
We all wear a mask or ask to be made whole
You told me your secrets
I traded them for gold
Took the gold
Melted it down
Wrapped it in love
Around and around
What was lost is now found?
As I lay here
In the ground
No longer existing

That's one of my favorite poems I've ever written, seeing how it helped me to get over a hurtful relationship in the past. What I took from it the most was how we all seem to exist in our own personal states of love. I would say it's best to enter a stage where you don't settle or just simply exist in your relationships. It's best if you become more conscious of what you seek out of a relationship and a significant other. The best way to describe how I feel about love and any relationship can be summed up in one word (legacy.)

What I mean by legacy is everyone should be building a bond to be looked back on and admired for its essence and truth.

Leisure Time

Have you ever seen a couple who have no problem spending all their time together? Trust me when I tell you it's a very hard thing to watch. The funny part about certain couples who spend all their time together is they become the same person once they've been together for so long. What I mean by they become the same person is they get on the same wave length channel. A couple who spends all their time together knows each other better than anyone. Personally I believe anyone who spends a majority of their time with their significant others promote and produce healthy bonds. But I would also say the type of things you do together with your significant other should always mean something to the both of you. I believe most people who spend a majority of their time together are unaware of how significant spending positive time with one another can fuel the relationship for the better. Maykayla and I both like the same things when it comes to spending leisure time together, these things include: bowling, attending the movies, dancing, relaxing at home, having water balloon fights with the kids, helping others rebuild houses, and a collection of things to challenge our sense of leisure time. Sometimes it serves a better purpose to have an outside perspective on life, love, and family. Spending positive leisure time outside the relationship has the power to advance your emotions, financial gains, mental capacities, etc. etc.

  As you grow yourself, and connect with your family members, what you begin to see is the connection between your inner child, and adult self coming back to life. I remember reaching a point in my life when I didn't laugh and show any kind of natural emotions. After serving 16 years in a state penitentiary I can accredit a lot of my change to Denver University Prison Arts Initiative founded by Dr. Ashley Hamilton, which gave me a sense of truth, love, and a beautiful sense of friendship. Also I would like to say Bridges to Life gave me a greater sense of understanding and empathy to take into the future. Another movement which is currently impacting my life is being a mentor for P.E.A.K (Peer Education Adjustment Keepers) has given me a platform to enhance my skills and reach many hearts who desire to truly change. Honestly I must give the credit to a combination of great people who had the courage to get involved with my life, and challenge me to better than I use to be. I believe leisure time is very important, but more significantly do we find how precious time is altogether. Time, as we know it to be true, is the most vital element known to mankind, and we spend a majority of our lives throwing it away every chance we get. As a dear friend of mine by the name of Louis Lopez always says "time is like water on a hot scorching day, you don't recognize how precious it is until you really need it." There are a lot of things you can do to have fun in your leisure time like the bowling alley, attending football games, and going as fast as you can around the skating rink. I also believe in working out with your significant other which serves two greater purposes. The first purpose it serves in your relationship is the two of you accomplish something together by getting physical fit. The other thing you accomplish is spending time quality time together, which is always well needed in every relationship.

My mom said "you need to get a better job." My mom makes better apple pie than you." My mom said "we need to go see a marriage counselor."

What!!!

Listen here you mom-huggers, it's nothing personal but your mother is not a part of your relationship. You may want her to be, but she is not. We're very thankful for all that mother does for us. She is beautiful, helpful, and well-needed in our family…but her nose doesn't belong all in our business. How do I tell my mother-in-law to back off? Move to Kansas.

Nah! Seriously it's best if you and your mate sit her down and calmly say "mom we love you very much but you have to let work through your own stuff."

Ask your mother-in-law what kind of relationship she had with her mother-in-law? If she doesn't listen to your word of advice, then you move to Kansas.

Recently, I was privileged to attend and graduate this course entitled Alternative to Violence at D.R.D.C which taught me that apologizing to our loved ones was something that needed to be done in order to restore the bond. I took what I learned and applied it here to because I feel my public apology was beyond due, and well needed. I remember feeling a large amount of guilt for hurting all the hearts I hurt, and treating young women the way I did. I told myself if I ever got the chance to apologize publicly I would do it to the best of my ability and make it special. Here are a few tips to help you apologize to anyone you've harmed or hurt in the past.

1. Prepare yourself to apologize to the person you feel you've harmed or cause hurt too.
2. Start by writing a few things on a piece of paper you would like to apologize for.

3. Be mindful of your tone when you apologize to the person you've harmed or caused hurt too.

4. Listen to what they are saying after you apologize.

5. Don't judge them for what they might say to you.

6. Do not expect a sense of resolve automatically after you apologize. Give them time to process your apology.

Is there someone you wish you could apologize too?

_____

_____

If you could apologize to this person whom you've hurt or harmed, how would you begin your apology?

_____

_____

"When you apologize to someone you've hurt or harmed you free yourself from many states of guilt"

Tecarra Lee Graham

A Silent Argument

A Guide To Understanding Your Mate, And Yourself A Little Bit Better

Imagine if you and your significant other had an argument with one another, but you couldn't use any words. I'm not the smartest person in the whole world, but I'm pretty sure a silent argument would look outlandish to anyone watching it. The moment you and your significant other begins to argue silently, I believe you'll see what you're arguing about has no merit to it. If we take a look throughout history, it's evident to explore how many arguments have transformed our daily lives. The majority of individuals who engage in arguments only want to be right instead of being happy. Sometimes we expect our significant others to be completely perfect, which is the craziest thing in the world. Without any sense of doubt we all know arguments are destine to occur in our relationships, but how we challenge ourselves to take care of one another during these disagreements is the key to understanding. When you've done wrong, and are made aware of your wrong doings how well are you at admitting and making amends to your significant other?

. Poorly

. Average

. Above Average

If you could change the outcome of every argument you've ever had in your life what would you have done different?

"Every argument doesn't have to end with a winner or a loser, sometimes you can tie"

Christopher Taylor
Also known as "CT"

A Guide To Understanding Your Mate, And Yourself A Little Bit Better

Chapter Six: Purpose

Nothing Personal

Throughout my many years as a peer mentor, I can't tell you how many individuals I've had to say this to. If someone does not meet your expectations in life and love don't take it so personal. I know what you're saying and I whole heartedly agree with you, it's easier said than done not taking certain things in relationships personal. One of these things I've noticed a lot of men take quite personal is the fact their significant other makes more money than they do. Its evident gentlemen it's a whole new world where equality isn't just another word to be thrown around. Truthfully you would think most men would be conditioned to women being in charge seeing how women run the world…they just let us think we are in charge. Whenever you begin to see your significant other as an equal partner, and balanced provider you'll be able to challenge those past ideologies you've grown accustom too. But the fact is you're not alone anymore when it comes to the financial side of your relationships, unless you want it that way.

Humorously I find myself quite entertained when telling others not to take things so personal in relationships because at one time I was the king of taking things personal. I asked myself a few years ago what kind of man I perceive myself to be. Am I the kind of guy who cries at the first sight of problematic tension? Am I someone who can't seem to stand up straight to save my life? The momma boy, who refuses to grow up and be a man is that me? (That's definitely not me). Am I the kind of guy who gets high and drunk every chance I get? The kind of guy that you would be embarrass to go out with simply because I make a fool of myself every where- causing you to regret meeting me in the first place. Are my eyes always blood shot red, staring at you with a goofy looking glare in my eyes? (Can't say that sounds like me either). Maybe I'm one of them crazy guys who seem to be cool, but at the first sign of disturbance I flip out and become some kind of mad man. Am I always wired up like a ticking time bomb, waiting to go off at the blink of an eye? (That's not me at all, but I do stand up for what I believe in, and refuse to compromise my principles). O.k. I got it. I'm the kind of guy who can't stop chasing tail no matter what! I'm the greedy man who licks his tongue out at every little hot thing I see in the grocery store. Thinking I'm some kind of player who can't tell the difference between a good woman and a loose goose tramp in the streets. (As entertaining as that sounds, that's not me either). The truth is I'm just someone who had to figure out what kind of man I wanted to be, just like many young men in the world. But the key to my success rest solely upon my own shoulders, as if you didn't know that already. Rory Aktins once told me something I'll never forget, he said "the moment you discover who you want to be is the day you'll believe it for yourself." I feel that by knowing who you are or understanding who you are striving to be you'll create a greater sense of purpose in your heart. I challenge all my fellow men to wake up every day to become better men than we were the day before. One of the first lessons I learned in life was how realistic life can be. Life is a very realistic entity as you may have grown to known. This is funny to hear myself describe life from a different perspective at this point in time. Due to my challenging upbringing I use to describe life as a cold cruel entity – which it definitely can be sometimes, but there are also good moments in life that present peaceful outlooks. Have you asked yourself why you may or may not over look these moments in your life? It's clear we sometimes create and expect our fallacies to come to life when the truth is sometimes things don't always work out the way we desire them too. Sometimes, even in relationships, we have to wake up to face the world as it is instead of how we believe it should be (truth). By accepting this unexpected nature life throws at us we are granted a very rare privilege to be better and form a conscious outcome that we succumb too.

      Have you ever been a victim of domestic violence? I can't truly speak on this topic too much seeing how I've never been a victim of domestic violence myself nor have I ever had any confrontations involving any domestic affairs. I can say I have many friends who have been the victim's of domestic violence and sexual assault. I would like to express to them how much I respect them and honor their strength which inspires me to always treat others the way I desire to be treated. Many people are very misinformed about the many issues surrounding DV cases and other forms of physical and verbal abuse. The truth is domestic violence has grown to be not only a national problem, but a global problem that screams "don't walk away from me!" here is a poem I wrote a few years ago for my friend who was beaten by her boyfriend, but remained strong and is now living a better life with God in her heart. "**At Last**"

> Living on the arms of destiny
> Holding time within the memories long gone
> Words have a way of fading into darkness
> Leaving us all alone
> A cross between today and tomorrow
> Burning ashes from afar
> Black as the night altogether
> Decorated by a million stars
> We don't see them from here
> Such a formal way of saying goodbye
> Words mean nothing to us on paper
> Until they meet the inner eye
> The eyes tell the heart
> The heart moves entirely too fast
> But the soul says
> Rest easy My Beautiful One
> You'll find peace and happiness
> At last

"Sometimes we find the end is just the beginning and the beginning is what we've been waiting for."

A Guide To Understanding Your Mate, And Yourself A Little Bit Better

I believe self –power plays a very important part in our everyday lives. I have dear friend and family member of mine who loves to challenge my perspective when asking questions about life and love. We find ourselves discussing relationship questions a lot, as if we were on a professional debate team about love. She has a grand perspective on how she sees love and I have a totally different perspective which challenges her entire way of life. No matter what I can truly say our bond is always unique and true, even though it has a mind of its own, I enjoy the beauty of having someone as true as her on my side.

Another beautiful bond I would say inspired me to be better in life and love is the bond of my older brother Ronald Frye and Suzanne Gomez. When I find myself looking at their bond, I am brought to a quiet state in my heart. It's as if my heart is saying **WOW**!

I must say in this day and age I am still amazed to see a bond beautiful as their type of bond. Most people fall in "like" nowadays, but to see two individuals I know from my family who are truly in love is like seeing a unicorn in the wild (not likely). My brother Ronald Frye is someone who has shown me so much in my lifetime, and I believe he is someone who the world has yet to discover as a rare entity. I recall a time when him and I were just two guys with a dream of being authors. That dream of ours seemed to formulate out of thin air, but we made it possible with the help of God. Ronald and I find ourselves discussing self-power and ambition a lot in our daily journeys. We find ourselves questioning what is it about having an inner power which makes mankind seek happiness.

William S. Graham and Maykayla Scott

We Think Alike

You know the funny thing about a mirror; it only reflects what is seen. Some of you poor unfortunate creatures are married to your mirror mate. You ask, what the hell is a mirror mate? A mirror mate is someone who is just like you in all aspects. Meaning if you like to flirt and be the center of intention, your mirror mate does too. It brings a smile to my heart when I think how much Maykayla and I reflect one another. It's almost like we've lived the same life, just in different bodies.

Often we hear how opposites attract one another, but not always. In some rare cases, it is the similarities that fire-up the old crock pot. If you are stubborn and bull-headed, it's not a shocker if your mirror mate refuses to due away with his old dingy college t-shirt. Screaming go Georgia Tech! Here are your most compatible astrological signs. Aries (March 21- April 19) who is often strong minded with an alluring personality can be a little clingy and competitive is most compatible with Aquarius, Sagittarius, Leo, and Gemini. Taurus (April 20- May 20) is most compatible with Virgo and Pisces. Taurus people have strength beyond their own imagine and understanding. The strength inside of a Taurus goes will with the Virgo who longs to explore the world and wonder about the curiosities of love. Also the character of Taurus compliments the determination hidden deep in Pisces who enjoys seeing anything which gives them power and purpose. Then there's sweet, sweet Gemini (May 21- June 20) who present a challenge to know and win over, but when you do break through to any Gemini you have them forever. Gemini is most compatible with the free flowing Aquarius and the balance of Libra. Cancer (June 21- July 22) is most compatible with Scorpio and Pisces. Cancer is the first sign to get caught up in some drama and create a strong sense of jealousy. But the Cancer is a very romantic sign who takes the likes of love more serious than most other signs. Just like Cancer there is another proud sign that sees love from a different perspective. Leo (July 23- Aug 22) is compatible with Sagittarius, Libra, Gemini, and Aries. Its true Leos are very head strong being the lions of the zodiac so it's best if they are with signs that enjoy challenging their heart on another level of love. Virgo (Aug 23 – Sept. 22) knows the meaning of love in ways only a few can comprehend. Taurus and Capricorn understand the love language spoken by Virgo and finds delight in creating the beauty of emotions together. Of course there's the true balance of Libra (Sept. 23- Oct. 22) sign of some of the most entertaining people of our times like rock and roll hall of fame star Chuck Berry, Drake, Toni Braxton, Ashanti, Young Jeezy, Dwayne Carter also known as Lil Wayne, Tip Harris (T.I.), Eminem, and the President Jimmy Carter who has the exact same birthday as myself Oct. 1. The signs Libras are most compatible with are Leo, Sagittarius, Scorpio, Aquarius, and Gemini. Each one of these signs challenges the balance of Libra to seek greater and compliment the relationship. Scorpio is the mysterious sign of all zodiac, full of happiness when power of union meets the beauty of truth and justice. Maykayla is a true Scorpio at heart and it's such a delightful thing to see how her mind works when faced with problems and a greater sense of love. The fearless nature of all the signs compatible with Scorpio is Pisces, fellow Scorpios, and Libras. The beautiful likes of Sagittarius (Nov. 22- Dec. 21) who is compatible with Leo, Aries, Aquarius, and Libra, finds peace in knowing how true love makes them better. 9 times out 10 if you see a Sagittarius they're smiling from ear to ear with a delightful sense of joy in their life. Capricorns (Dec. 22- Jan. 19) have a great sense of being right and getting straight to the point. They truly dislike anyone who wastes their time, patience is short with a Capricorn (don't be the one who gets yelled at.) Because they are so strong minded and outspoken, Capricorns are mostly compatible with Pisces, Scorpio, Virgo, and Taurus. The sign that appraises freedom the most is the water sign of Aquarius (Jan. 20- Feb. 18). Because of this, the desire to be with other signs that understand how freedom works is very important. Usually you'll find Aquarius in relationships with the signs of Gemini or Libra, two other signs designed to give light to being unrestricted. Pisces (Feb. 19- March 20) are the true heart throbs of the zodiac. Most people feel that all the other signs provide a greater sense of love, but the truth is when you're in love with a Pisces you'll know what true love feels like. Sometimes Pisces can get caught up in the details so much they overlook the humor in life and love.

    Be honest with yourself, are you the type of person who stares at your neighbor's hot smoking wife? Or the hunky guy next door you keep smiling at? You are a victim of the "juicy eyes syndrome"
    Everything seems good from a distance, but that doesn't mean it's good for you. Everything meant for

your neighbor belongs to your neighbor. It is not designed for you.

Trust me when I tell you, if your significant other takes care of you and treats you right, there's nothing better than that. Please don't make a fool yourself thinking the party is elsewhere, when the truth is you're quite blessed to have a loving mate (I think). The party is where you make the party. Or better yet, you are the party. If your relationship seems to be getting a little dry- spice it up. Reach higher for something besides ordering take out, watching movies, and living basic.

"Take a chance and dance to the beat of life"

Say you're the kind of person who enjoys your own personal space. There's nothing wrong with that. You may feel living with someone complicates your situation. Maybe you snore loud enough to wake up the whole neighborhood, and you don't want to subject that torture to anyone else. I get it.

The only problem with that is humans are very affectionate creatures. We like to be as close as possible to the things we love.

Having that said, you know what comes next. Congratulations!

You're getting a room mate. It's only a matter of time before your play station goes in a box to collect dust.

Nah! Seriously it's best if you and your mate sit her down and calmly say "mom we love you very much but you have to let work through our own stuff."

Ask your mother-in-law what kind of relationship she had with her mother-in-law? If she doesn't listen to your word of advice, then you move to Kansas.

Say you're the kind of person who enjoys your own personal space. There's nothing wrong with that. You may feel living with someone complicates your situation. Maybe you snore loud enough to wake up the whole neighborhood, and you don't want to subject that torture to anyone else. I get it.

The only problem with that is humans are very affectionate creatures. We like to be as close as possible to the things we love.

Having that said, you know what comes next. Congratulations!

You're getting a room mate. It's only a matter of time before your play station goes in a box to collect dust.

A Guide To Understanding Your Mate, And Yourself A Little Bit Better

Heaven on Earth

I tell you no lie
Heaven sounds pretty good
With roads made of milk and honey
And everyone doing what they should
But I must say
I feel guilty
Mainly because when I look at you
I smile
In your arms I'm comfortable
It's like being next to a cloud
You're definitely an angel
Watching me at all times
Giving me your true love
With all the matching signs
To be honest with you
I know beautiful entities are what they are worth

**And this is forever true
I'm just blessed to say I found my own personal heaven right here on earth...with you**

Remembering …

Looking back over the years, my hearts recollects how many memories we've shared. Each memory warms my heart to its core. You are someone who understands my kind of love. Someone who doesn't judge me, or Make me feel unwanted in our bond. If I died today, I can honestly say the times spent with you were well worth it. This is me remembering us…

It wasn't raining

Not a cloud in the sky
But I felt gloomy
I didn't know why?
Oh yes I do
I remember why?
Because I had no one to love
No reason to fly
So there I was…walking down the street
Head down in a state of defeat
Something told me to look up
I did

A Guide To Understanding Your Mate, And Yourself A Little Bit Better

It was you
 Glowing like angel
Beautiful and true
I wanted to speak
I could not say a word
You said "hello" to me
I couldn't hear one word
But I knew you were beautiful
I knew you were divine
I knew you were bold

I knew I wanted you to be mine
I knew we were family
I knew God had a design
I knew you were crazy like me
I knew I was blind
I knew I had to find your love
I knew it was time
To meet an angel

"Thank you for all that you do for me. I could never fully pay you back, but I could love you with all of my heart. I will give you a light to always see. With love in my heart I say today, tomorrow, and forever…it will be you and me."_____

-

I am a firm believer of fairness and equality. It's not my fault, I'm a Libra. Anyway, it is very important to play fair in your relationships. I know this should be a nobrainier type of subject, but it's not. The truth is a lot of couples live in unbalanced relationships, which eventually results in departure.

Here's an example: say you've been to work all day and you come home to see your mate sitting on the couch. You don't panic as you gradually make your way to the kitchen area. You look in the sink to spot a dirty dinner plate accompanied by a fork. You still don't quite panic. Another look into the oven and refrigerator reveals what you knew already- somebody isn't playing fair.

Fairness is a very vital thing in every relationship. Fairness feels good knowing someone has your back, and they long to pull their fair share in a partnership.

For example: say your significant other wanted you to sit down and watch figure skating with them. Would you act like you had prior engagements in order to dodge something you didn't desire to watch? Remember playing fair consist of you seeing your partner as a significant other, and as an equal. The moment you fail to see them in that light, is the beginning stage of a devastating relationship.

Here's a list of things you might experience

Near death experience
Retirement
Chronic illness
Spouse dying
Beloved friend dies
Moving to a new location
Pet dies
Child dies
Unfaithful spouse

Loss of home
Infertility
Division
Abandonment
Drug problems
Neglect

As we take a look at this list, I am very aware some of us are struggling with one, if not more than one, of these heart aches.
The ability to overcome the things that try to knock us down is something we all grow to respect. Not to sound like some kind of school cheerleader, but you can do it! Yes you can! You can do it, make a plan!
Seriously though, I understand how life deals us crappy hands, but we must remember how strong we are.

Balance = Love

They say in life it is healthy to seek complete balance
To know someone loves you enough to tell you the truth
To understand the level of their care
To walk with them
Talk with them and stay with them through hard times or less
To be someone special in their life
Supporting them as much as possible
To share a grand state of laughter with them
Know their pitfalls

Trust their judgment
Grow in time with them
To be perfect as one
Weighing out their inner truth
To be bounded by care
To work hard
Know relaxation
Be as beautiful as you can be
Remembering the times to come
With love, life, and loyalty

As we've grown to understand a healthy state of balance is well-needed in every relationship we encounter what it means to be equal to our significant others. Maykayla and I both agree that creating a heavy sense of balance is one of the most important elements in any relationship. The funny part is we don't always agree with one another on every issue, but we do see eye to eye on many heartfelt things. When I wrote this passage I wanted to capture my Libra essence, and depict what true balanced resembled. I know personally if I don't have balance in my life and relationships I am a complete mess. Maykayla said having balance in her life and relationships are equal to freedom. I believe respecting your significant other's opinions and feelings are only part of demonstrating the balance the two of you have for one another. Surely you would agree the moment you respect something or someone for who they are or for what they feel, you gather a better perspective of their inner self. Damon "The Nomad" Davis author of Voices in the Cellar and Parenting beyond Tragedy (A Male's Perspective) always says "creating perfect balance in your relationship is an art even Bruce Lee would have admired."

William S. Graham and Maykayla Scott

A Guide To Understanding Your Mate, And Yourself A Little Bit Better

Chapter Seven: Precious

The Sunset

Today I seen a sunset
Beautiful and rare
It melted my heart
I wish you were there
Only if I could have shared that moment with you
To stare into your eyes and enjoy your smile
I would have told you how your love reminds me of a cloud
Soft, beautiful, and divine
Do you mind if I tell you something?
I love your time
Time is precious
Each second you have is yours
So when you give it to someone you love
 Someone you adore
Understand it's like a sunset,
Giving you back more

Maykayla wrote this poem highlighting how many people overlook the small things in life like a beautiful sunset or a flowing river. When I first read this poem from her I was amazed how much it spoke to me, seeing how I have a bad habit of forgetting to stop and smell the roses on a daily basis. The part that really attracted my heart was how connected the sunset and the person you love are as one. For some odd reason I thought about all the couples who have to say goodbye to their mates due to performing service duties or jobs which require them to be away from each other for long periods of time. Nonetheless I believe if you take the time to sit back and enjoy the little things in life, you might be shocked to discover what weighs quite heavy upon your heart.

Is Cheating Worth It

If we take a close observation into our daily culture we see how many individuals refuse to grasp the magnitude of what it means to be faithful. Personally, I can speak for myself when I say I was very selfish and completely unaware of all the hurt I caused others. I remember the first time I cheated on a young lady in grade school, which seemed like a billion years ago. Any way I recall leaning up against my school locker in the hallway as the young lady questioned why I chose to lie to her and break her heart? At the time I thought it was quite cute to have a young lady crying over me, saying to myself I **must be some kind of player or Mac daddy.** I was very immature back then and partially insecure to discover I had to hurt young women to feel wanted. At the time I couldn't give her the young lady an explanation why I chose to break her heart and lie to her. Many years later I realized I had major trust issues when it came to women. I can't say it enough, seeing how most young men suffer from this same perspective growing up. Why do you think this is so? Truthfully I believe most men feel they can't trust the judgments of most women for a numerous of reasons. A distant look into our past would reveal the ugly truth why most men do not trust the judgment of most women. Some would proclaim the origin stems all the way back to Adam and Eve, and the poor judgment demonstrated in the Garden of Eden. Others would say most men are brain washed to believe women are easily compromised through persuasion. This is a very sexist way of thinking, I agree, but this way of thinking is promoted and perpetuated everyday. This is quite ironic seeing how most men are the ones who get caught cheating or (compromised). Not saying women don't cheat themselves because they do, but women are sneakier than men and that is another character trait that gets promoted falsely. Or is it true? Are women sneakier than men? I refuse to answer that question (one) because I really don't know who is sneakier between women or men. The second reason why I want answer that question is because I don't want to get punched in the eye by all the women in the world. (I'm a smart guy). But the bigger question is why do people cheat? I've reviewed this question over and over in my mind, which produced many results but I care to dig a little more on such a touchy subject. Is it safe to say people cheat because they are in search of the diamond bond? It's no mystery to discover most people admire diamonds for their surface value the same way most people admire relationships for what they feel they can attain out of them. I'm sure we've all heard the term "gold digger" or "sugar daddy" and "sugar mama" right! These are terms that describe an agreement between two or more people who understand the bond they possess is a superficial stage front. Usually in these types of bonds gifts are exchanged from one subject to another, and favors are returned to person who donates. I want even sit here and lie to you and say I haven't had a few sugar mamas in my day. At one point in time I had about 6 sugar mamas giving me gifts for favors, which some came in the simplest form of attention. But here's something I will tell you dear world, if you're entering any relationship with high hopes of attaining something superficial you're in for a confusing twist. The superego may allow you to attain what you perceive to be true or what you believe will bring you happiness, but the truth is you sell a piece of your soul every time you trade affection for gold. The base of this passage highlights how cheating sometimes isn't worth what we perceive to be true, it's only in our heads. Trust me when I tell you it's wiser to work on your relationship or just simply be honest and tell your mate the truth (you aren't happy). Have you ever cheated on someone and felt it wasn't worth it after you cheated? How did it make you feel? If you could take it back would you? In better news according to the CDC, the divorce rate in the United States is 3.2 per 1,000 people. That rate decreased by 18% between 2008 and 2016, despite the fact declining indications show both marriage and divorces are unfathomable to certain portions of the population. The current statistics for the United States show half of all marriages end in divorce. Seemly that may be presented as true at some period in time, but that's outdated information. The truth is divorce rates are quite lower than projected.

"The wisdom of love is a fore thinking not an after thought"

The Attributes of a True Man

In deep thought I understand the error of my past ways. With a question lingering deep in my soul I ask what does it mean to be a man? Let me tell you what I thought a man was in my diluted state of mind. I thought a man was someone who had a penis, and walked around with his chest poked out. Recognizing the ignorance of my past self, I forced myself to acknowledge the definition of a true man. I discovered a man takes responsibility within his heart without a cast of doubt- knowing what needs to be done in order to succeed. A boy lies down with a woman or young woman, creates a child and walks away. A boy avoids responsibility simply because he knows he's not ready to become a man. Boys are unprepared and truly not equip to take on the qualities of being a man. A man knows the definition of sacrifice, developing a stage of independence within his heart he can be proud about. A man holds his head up when making divine decisions that affect his future. A man does not let anyone alter his process when making these decisions, unless, he can see the positive perspectives which inner line with his divine purpose as well. A man knows what he has to do in order to keep himself and his family afloat. A man does this without boasting, bragging, or show boating altogether. A man can see his pitfalls, in which he learns from without having to repeat the same mistakes over and over again. A man's sole purpose is to be an example for his family, the next generation, and the likes of all mankind. A man doesn't have all the answers to all the questions in life, but if he is ignorant to a subject which serves his best benefit he will allow himself to be educated or learn what he must to gather a better understanding of the subject. Once those answers have been attained, a man will inspire those around him to learn thus such knowledge as well. A man makes all things around him greater or he challenges all things around him to grow in one form or another. A man takes a sense of honor in knowing he did the right thing in producing a hard day of work. A man provides and prefers to show his love through actions and takes his time to explain those actions with words of encouragement and trust. A man grows to value love and respects the rights of having money, grooming himself to be presentable, and having gallant attributes. A man understands adulthood to the fullest, refusing to carry himself outside of the defining character which classified him a man in the first place. A man takes the love of an understanding woman or mate and honors it the fullest of his capabilities within his heart. If the woman a man chooses is unaware of his true potential he finds it to be his duty to illuminate his attributes. A man builds a home with his family; in which each one of his beloved family members hold equal parts in the stake of the home, and enjoys the fruits of his labor. A man knows what he needs to do, as he keeps his eyes on his goals and ambitions. A man believes in his abilities, and strives to see his dreams fulfilled through devotion and faith. A man searches his heart, exploring his soul in search of knowledge to feed his resourceful mind. The attributes of a true man is allowing the affects of life to show him how deep it actually goes.

"A man only fears the unknown, but takes a divine purpose in exploring what the unknown has to offer"

Everett M. Harrington

William S. Graham and Maykayla Scott

A Guide To Understanding Your Mate, And Yourself A Little Bit Better

Chapter Eight: Protection

A Couple's Finances

Would you prefer your finances to be together or separate as a couple?

Why or why not?

I was watching the news the other day, which stated couples who have a combined bank account trust each other a lot more than couples who have separate accounts. I thought to myself I don't know how true that study reads, but I would agree financial problems cause a lot of break ups in every relationship. Even some of the greatest music groups of our time have broken up behind disputes surrounding money. Maykayla gave me a very deep perspective on this subject by saying "I don't believe couples who are married shouldn't have separate bank accounts because it just looks strange." I asked her to expound on this subject further when she said "it looks strange for married couples to have separate bank accounts?" Maykayla said "I believe if you love someone you must love them without guard rails or barricades of burdens on your heart." She continued "that's not to say go into every relationship guaranteeing success because when you do that life will see to it you fail for being a know it all." "Anyone and everyone in a relationship should take the time to study their mate or significant other. Not just for research purposes, but hopefully to help your significant other if you see them struggling with an issue. Like for example if you recognize your mate or significant other stumbles home 3 days of a week smelling like a Irish bar tender, you might want to be vigilant if this future problem keeps occurring. The major problem with most couples is they sit back, afraid to self correct their significant other's habits or misconducts. Then they are the first ones to scream I told you so when the whole family is camping out at your brother-in-law's place for two years. When it comes to finances, the water from the river should always reach the ocean. What this means is the minute the river dries up the ocean pays for it severely."

Proverbs 24:3

By wisdom a house is built, and through understanding it is established; through knowledge its rooms are filled with rare and beautiful treasures.

"The moment you become uncomfortable in your own skin is the day you pretend to be who you wish you were."

Kelly Bruce

Family and Friends

I swear if I had a list for every family member or friend who gave someone some bad relationship advice the line would stretch around the block. The truth is everyone believes they're Dr. Phil when it comes to giving out relationship advice. Everyone knows family members and friends are the first ones to spew out some relationship advice to you which is designed to mess up your relationship. It's almost like family members and friends intend to make your relationship more complicated with their useless advice. Then to add injury to insult you discover they are either not in a relationship themselves or their relationship is in the dumps. I once read this quote which stated "everyone seems to be genius until you take their words of advice and discover you've been talking to a fool." To point is no matter how convincing your friend's advice seems to be, don't listen to what they're saying- it's all hokum. My dear friend and family member Patricia Riley tells me all the time "don't listen to people's advice; they'll mess up your relationship every time." I believe family and friends have righteous intentions whenever they try to give you relationship advice, but professional help is a lot different than recommended advice. I remember a time when I listened to a friend's advice pertaining to an issue I was having with a girlfriend in high school. The issue was about my girlfriend and I spending more quality time together, I was on the basketball team and football team at the time. My girlfriend was very understandable about those extra curriculum activities, but she didn't understand why I chose to hang out with my friends in late night clubs. My friend's advice was to dump my girlfriend because she wanted to hold my success back, and I would be better off without her. Later in life I discovered how I made an irrational decision by breaking up with her, but I remember my friend who gave me the advice to dump her dating my ex girlfriend. I was quite upset for a long time about what had occurred between the two of us, but I was taught a very valuable lesson about taking other people's advice especially family and friends. My dear friend Christopher Miller once told me something his father (Bobbi Miller) told him when it comes to family and friends. He said "you have to be willing to take people's advice, and throw it in the trash when they walk away like when people who ask you to taste their nasty food, but you know they can't cook."

Proverbs 27:6

Wounds from a friend can be trusted, but an enemy multiplies kisses.

Love Concurs All

I found myself
Only to lose myself
Only to rediscover myself
Only to doubt myself
Only to hug myself
Only to need myself
Only to lie to myself
Only to tell myself the truth
Only to forget myself
Only to be myself
Only to love myself
Love concurs all

A Guide To Understanding Your Mate, And Yourself A Little Bit Better

Maykayla Scott

While writing this poem I discovered how each line was actually a stage or some form of emotion I endured. I believe a lot of people go through these same emotions in their lifetime. It's almost like we as humans have to endure these emotions in order to add value to our journey toward love. I use to tell myself no one understands my form of love, I was convinced. Have you ever felt like everyone you've ever dated is just practice for the real thing which prepares you for the depths of true love? I know I have, and it's quite outstanding to embody what true love has in store for the diligent heart. I told William a few months ago I believe love is an entity of divine measures unfathomable to the unconscious heart. I expound on that further by saying if we take a look at love from a perspective of warriors, who honor the soul of battle. I believe love is the same way, honoring every couple who is willing to struggle in the name of love, and endure whatever comes with the battles of affection. Before meeting William I had a refined way of looking at diamonds, as if they had no flaws. William educated my mind by opening my eyes to how the pressure of life makes us, as humans, resemble diamonds. It's not that we are perfect in our journeys of refinement, that's definitely not the case. But what people consider marvelous is our will power to stay consistent to our bonds/purposes. I believe love only honors the people who are true at heart, and rewards the strength of time.

Masterpiece

I wish you could see what I see
If you could, surely, you would agree
You are a masterpiece
Beautiful from your head to your feet
Strong and opinionated
Graceful and unique
Understanding and trustworthy
No one could ever compete
Completely divine and truly refined at the least
I say this now and forever
You are something truly special to me
Forever you are my masterpiece

Doubt

    Regardless of the status of your relationship, everyone has a little doubt in their hearts at first. Having doubt in your relationship, in the beginning stages, is quite normal and nothing to feel ashamed about. How did you feel the first time you moved in with your significant other? Were you nervous or hesitant at first? Where you were respectful and overly polite to your significant other? Every couple has doubt at first, but after about 6 years of living together, how much of that changes or grows into relaxation? The only time you should worry about doubt is when you and your significant other have been a couple for quite some time. If you and your significant other still have a cloud of doubt in your relationship after a certain period of time, then you have issues. Maykayla said "the moment you become uncomfortable in your own skin is the day you pretend to be who you wish you were."

When I first read Maykayla's quote I thought about a time when I doubted my writing, as if I was ashamed of having feelings. Just like a lot of you who stuff your words, feelings, and thoughts down into your souls, afraid to give them a voice, I was the same way. The moment I discovered my voice it was like opening a flood gate of emotions I was waiting to express to someone. I believe most couples spend a majority of their quality time dodging important conversations which are needed to grow the relationship. The diamond bond forces couples who recognize they can improve their relationship to acknowledge the uncertainty within the connection. In every bond its best you understand how disconnect in your relationship may stem from a lack of communication or personal issues you are failing to address as a couple. It is also very important to know a lack of confidence stems from mistrust, uncertainties, and suspense. What I've noticed from my own personal experience is most couples nowadays fail to get to know each other. Ask yourself how well do I know my significant other? Let's take Maykayla and I, a Scorpio and a Libra, who share a lot of things in common, but also we strive to know one another's differences. What we all need to learn is every relationship is a give and take type of bond; sacrifice is well need in every bond, especially if you desire to have a diamond bond.

William S. Graham and Maykayla Scott

Chapter Nine: Property

Have you ever had a friend with an overly protective mother or father? The truth is I use to be very jealous of those types of kids, seeing how I didn't feel as if anyone cared for me enough to be overly protective. I recall making fun of all the kids who had overly protective parents or care givers, calling them babies and just hating. I shared this knowledge with you as a way of explaining how growing up some people take neglect or abandonment a little different than others. I believe every relationship takes a certain level of affection or quality time which is well needed to fuel the bond. Maykayla explained to me the other day how most couples view their relationships as property instead of free flowing bonds which are interchangeable. I wondered about that for a moment, asking myself how do people grow to own the relationships instead of being a part of the relationships. I once read this passage which stated "sometimes the things you own end up owning you as well." I believe that is a very important quote to remember when we think of all the couples who feel they own their relationships like property. But don't get me wrong, I believe there's a healthy way of owning your relationship and taking a certain level of pride in your bond. For example: just like your house you've worked hard for and care for dearly, you have a certain level of pride about your home right! Well if you look at your relationship or your bond the same way you view the pride you have for your beautiful home, you have a diamond bond in the making. Now the reason why I said you have a diamond bond in the making is because you have to be willing to take care of the bond the way you would take care of your beautiful home. So just to clarify what I'm saying ownership in a relationship is only healthy when you are willing to take care of the bond and share equal responsibilities. Despite what many people may say, coming home to an empty place of residence sucks very much. The thing about humans is we were designed to show and accept affection from others; it becomes our purpose to live. So imagine waking up every morning with everything you could ever dream of, but you don't have the one thing everyone desires and can't buy…true love. Someone once told me a few years ago his wife meant the world to him. I thought about their bond from his perspective, then asked myself a question (if the world, as I know it, was being destroyed tomorrow how would I react?) I wondered would I go and try to hide in a bunker somewhere. Or maybe I would spend as much time as possible with the people I love. The truth is we all find ourselves empty or clouded with loneliness from time to time. I recall mentoring a 19 year old kid who was homeless or suffered from mental health disorders. His eyes were emotionless as he explained an early life of loneliness. The kid explained to me how a series of events led up to him being homeless. I felt a level of empathy for him, as I flashed back to a time when I ran away from my foster home. The young kid and I connected from past struggles, and challenged one another to stay sharp going forward in life, and avoid growing dull or unconscious. He gave me a jewel to take forward in life that I'll share with you guys right now. He said "when you'll homeless you don't have anything but your free will, and that is the true definition of being rich." I told him I inspire to one day be a true rich man of value and love.

Sacrifice

What have you sacrificed in your relationship that you can look back on and feel a sense of pride about? What I mean by this is let's say if you and your significant other came to this country without a red cent in your pocket, and built your family business from the ground up, that's something to be proud about. Or maybe your significant other went off to war in which you had to hold down the household, only to discover your significant other has been injured in battle a few years later. When I see or hear about scenarios and situations like these in life, my heart is immediately touched by the will power and essence of love. I must admit earlier in my life I couldn't say I honored love from a perspective I now see it from. Maykayla and I would agree, love challenges us all to see if we are worthy of its essence, which a lot of people fall inadequate too. Maykayla and I would say if you look at your relationship, and see no signs of a struggle to overcome or endure you have a problem my friend. Regardless of what anyone would say to you, please understand there is no such thing as a perfect relationship or bond when dealing with true love. True love is designed to remind you of how precious it actually is, or has the power to be. But please understand Maykayla and I aren't saying you have to have a crisis beyond comprehension in order for you to be happy, no we're not saying that at all. What Maykayla and I are saying is if you have true love in your life, you'll know it by how hard you'll have to fight to keep it. Have you ever noticed how the couples in the lime light always seem to be perfect in our eye view? The truth is if we could see into their relationship, we would discover how the celebrities have problems just like we do, if not worst. I remember when I use to think people who were on television and on the magazines were in perfect relationships, and let me just say I was truly shocked to discover how normal they were under the scope of love. But I'll keep it honest by saying every time one of those couples in the public eye chooses to separate or get a divorce a little part of me loses hope in the arches of love. I believe we all relate to their bonds as an origin of affection because we want them to win, as if they were our favorite sports team or something. If your relationship was a sports team, what team would you compare it too? Would your relationship be the Denver Broncos? Who have a great traditional football history of support and hard nose fans. Would you say your relationship is a team in need of a win, seeing how it's been a while since your last championship? Well like a legendary coach once said "the only way to win is to play until the other team loses" I live by that creed everyday. What that creed has taught me is if you want your relationships to work out in life or love, you have to be willing to work at it constantly. If you truly look at your relationship, or past relationships, ask yourself how far were you willing to go in order to see the growth of the bond. I'll be honest with you by stating if you gave up at the first sign of trouble, or talked yourself out of helping the bond to be better, you have a lot to learn about love. As we acknowledge the root of love, it's best we recognize how some people interrupt their perspective of love incorrectly. What I mean by this is a lot of people give up on love because they don't know how real love should feel. I'm not ashamed to say I questioned what love is supposed to feel like. I believe we all have that lingering question residing in the pit of our hearts, saying what is love? I wrote a poem a few years ago called "What is Love?" and I would like to share it with you guys if you don't mind.

"What is Love?"

A word we say
Or something we're taught to say
Like how's your day?
Knowing we don't always mean it
So why do we say it?
Especially if it's not rooted in our hearts
But anyway
Maybe love is like a fire?
Burning us every chance it gets
Then we say "don't touch that!"
Telling others about how our scars at heart will never heal
Screaming to others "Love isn't real!"
We can't touch it
We can't see it
We can't even taste it…like air
But that doesn't stop anyone from breathing right
Maybe love is like a boat

Able to sail us away from our daily problems
The same problems that punch us in the face everyday
Shall we go cry in the corner?
Like the child who never knew love
Like the sun failing to shine
Like the words which echo back to self
Like the time forgotten
Like the beauty lost
Like the hurt unknown
Like what?
What is love?
A message from God
Saying what?
Just love.
Just love.
Just love.
Do we?

When I first wrote this poem I wanted to present a sarcastic perspective on how we approach the entity of love. I asked Maykayla how she felt about love and her answer was quite simple and to the point. She said "if I love anything or anyone, my actions will reflect my words.

When people's words don't reflect their actions, it's their way of saying (I don't care right now or maybe never did). I must admit I went so long only caring for myself inside the prison system I felt like I forgot how to love others.

Maykayla showed me how to stop avoiding my emotions and face them head on no matter the outcome.

Are there any emotional problems you tend to avoid in your daily life?

_____
_____

Why do you feel you avoid these emotions?

_____
_____

If you could go into a private room and say all the things you desire to say, what would you say?

_____
_____

The first time you said the words I love you, how did you feel saying it?

_____
_____

Do you remember who you said those beautiful words too?

_____
_____
_____
_____

Name five things you've learned about love over the years

_____
_____
_____

If I were to answer the question of what I learned about love I would say I learned how love can change the heart of a person. I can honestly say love has stepped into my life with patience when I wasn't ready to accept its essence. Love entered my life when my heart felt like it couldn't grow anymore or be anymore developed. Love gave me purpose when I wanted to sit in my prison cell and sulk at the world. Love told me secrets when everyone felt like I wasn't worthy of there ideas. Love befriended me when the world said you should die cold and alone in a dark prison cell. Love washed the dirt out of my eyes and told me to stop being blind to the beautiful entities of the world. Love showed me how a masterpiece of emotions wanted to be in my life, and give me the gifts of affection. Love opened its arms to hug me ever so tightly, and embrace my inner core for its faults and flaws. Love is God and everything in the face of grace.

Support and Stability

Regardless of what anyone tells you support and stability is a very important element in every relationship. I use to think support and stability was something people had to give to me, and I didn't have to reciprocate it. I learned many valuable lessons on that subject which helped me remember it's not always about me all the time. I can honestly say I had a collection of individuals who believed in my change and supported me and currently plays vital roles in my life. Maykayla says "the people in her life came directly from God, as a message to remind her how beautiful the grace has the power to change all perspectives." My best friend Ronald Frye makes me laugh when we talk about support and stability. He says "people forget how blessed we are at times, only seeing the pain of times and overlooking the blessing bestowed within our existence."

Ronald Frye served 22 years in Colorado Department of Corrections, before being released in 2015. He now resides in Denver, Colorado with his beloved wife Suzanne Gomez, who played a major role in publishing his first book entitled "God Can and God Will." I will say with an earnest heart Ronald Frye, Suzanne Gomez, and Patricia Riley serve as the dominating support system for Maykayla and I. We are forever thankful for their humble approach toward life and love.

"When you look around to see who's really riding with you, don't be surprised if the crowd is quite small"

Antonio "Baby Bounce" Stancil

William S. Graham and Maykayla Scott

Chapter Ten: Peace

Holy Matrimony

Like many young people from my decade I failed to see the significance of marriage. To be honest with the whole world I have yet to attend a wedding and I'm in my mid 30's. I don't know if I should be ashamed of humored at the fact I've never attended a holy matrimony of unity. But than again who's to say I'm wrong for viewing marriage in a standoffish way. I believe we as a culture put too much focus on the theatricalities of marriage instead of recognizing why we choose to marry in the first place. I can't tell you how many damaged marriages I've been a witness too. It's almost like we get married just to throw a party and eat some expensive cake in a room full of people we don't know (say cheese!) Maykayla and I were discussing marriage the other day and discovered neither of us likes the word divorce or separation. I told her it's clear to see we both have attachment issues due to how we were neglected as children. Which presented a great study to analyze how many couples disagree with divorce because of their childhood abandonment issues? How do you feel about marriage?

_____
_____
_____
_____

If you were to give some advice to a couple who has recently married, what would you like to tell them?

_____
_____
_____

In what areas could your marriage use some well needed work?

_____
_____

Name ten things you disagree with your significant other about.

1. _____

2. _____

3. _____

4. _____

5. _____

6. _____

7. _____

8. _____

9. _____

10. _____

Now as you review the list you just put together, ask yourself how much of these disagreements are worth fighting over? Then ask yourself how many of these disagreements reoccur in your daily relationship?

Someone once told me marriage is about give and take, the more you give the more they take. (I'm just kidding!)

But the truth is the moment you enter a union or bond with anyone, its best to remember how important the bond is as a collective whole. Most individuals approach their relationship from a one sided perspective, or they don't fully grasp what it means to work as a cohesive unit. The moment you and your significant other neglect your ability to work together, nothing in your bond will ever grow. It's a proven fact; most people enter relationships unaware of the responsibilities and liabilities that come with having a bond. It's just like when you're driving on the highway; you can't use your freedoms irresponsibly. So many people get caught up in the emotional baggage of their relationships, and neglect the other sides of adopting a heart felt bond.
Relationships, for the most part, are designed just like team sports. You may be a great contributor to your team, but the fact is you can't beat everyone. Michael Jordan is the greatest basketball player to grace a court, this is true, but without team mates he could not have accomplished all the great things that he did for the game. I believe once we begin to view our relationships in a better light, we'll grow to know true peace within our hearts. Marriage as we've grown to know it has suffered a costly blow to the heart and minds of many young generations. At times I feel a grave sense of

responsibility for such an outcome, and ask myself how I can help the dying art of love. My answer comes to me in the form of a parable "it is not the man who saves the world people remember, but the man who chooses to be a vital part of the world people never forget." What this parable is basically saying is I should worry less about changing others when I haven't ironed out my own wrinkles in my pants. During my travels of ink, there are a lot of strange things I've been asked to write, but I must say the oddest thing someone ever has asked me to write was their wedding vows. Don't worry strange guy out there I wouldn't never say your name because I'm a professional somewhat, but I will talk about the passage I wrote. When I first wrote it I asked myself I wonder how much of these words reflect in his heart compared to being just words to him when he reads it back to himself. Then I asked myself how was I able to create someone's vows, and not feel anything emotionally? I didn't know if I had trained my heart to be a writing machine or maybe I wanted to actually feel the words I was writing. I told myself when the day comes for me to write my vows it would be funny if I didn't have anything to say. (I doubt it, but it wouldn't be the first time right! wink, wink)

A Happy Median

I recall a metaphor my uncle told when I was 15 years old. He said "one thing you need to know about women, boy, is they live for the word compromise!" At the time I didn't have the slightest idea what he was talking about. I just remember saying to myself compromise is a big word for a man without a job, who

A Guide To Understanding Your Mate, And Yourself A Little Bit Better

drinks all day. Anyway years later I discovered a drunken man's wisdom has fruitful merits as well. Seeing how I found myself in a position with an irritate girlfriend who thought it would be a wonderful idea to run a butcher knife through my sternum. She had warned me several times about my cheating on her, and how she wasn't going to continue to put up with me disrespecting her. I knew she meant business so I didn't play around with her heart anymore. Our personal compromise resulted in me getting as far as I could away from her-she kindly obliged me. Even though that story isn't the best example to highlight the definition of compromise, you understand what I'm getting at. It's no mystery to discover the male ego struggles with compromise the most. The word compromise to the male ego means give up, weak, inadequate, or surrender. I get it; I use to be the same way before I grew to understand the power in the person who chooses to compromise compared to the person who loses everything in vain. In the bible it says "pride comes before the fall," this is definitely true. I use to fancy myself the king of pride back in the day. This same pride caused me a lot of pain every time I allowed it to get out of control. If you long to see process in your relationship, the word compromise needs to become your best friend. Most people understand the word median means being in the middle or in intermediate position. I like to think of the word median in a relationship means the middle of the bed, a place you won't be sleeping if you do not learn to compromise with your significant other. Maykayla says if you don't view your marriage or relationship as a business deal, you don't understand what it means to compromise. If you want peace in your home and heart you must be willing to compromise, or meet your significant other in the middle. Lesson number one will be when the two of you make the decision to move in together. I'll tell you right now, if you aren't ready to compromise in your relationship, you'll discover how fast your feelings get hurt by someone you love.

"True love forces everyone to meet in the middle, how you get there is up to you"
Author and Publisher, Robert Graham

What Do You Need?

The other day Maykayla asked me a very profound question. She said "how come men don't tell women exactly what they need?" I thought about her question for a brief second then responded kindly with "I don't know!" A few days later I was able to give her a well thought out answer. I'll generalize what I told her by stating "I can't speak for the entire race of men but I can provide you with an in depth look into the indoctrination of a young black male. Growing up in Carolina and thus such regions, I will admit I wasn't raised to need a woman for too much. This way of thinking as you know it has become a dinosaur train of thought, but note I did not invent what I was affected by. People trip me out when I say things like "I was taught not to need a woman for too much of nothing, and be the sole provider of the family" as if I'm the one who invented the way things were back in the recent day of time. I am just like every other enlightened man who understands oppression and challenges my own indoctrinations daily. I challenge these indoctrinations because I do not desire to hold down anything or anyone who has the ability to rise above their current conditions." I would agree that most couples need to understand how important communication has the power to affect the relationship. Every relationship is built on the arches of communication and compassion.

Breaking Up

I know this passage sucks, but we have to address it nonetheless. First I'll start by stating the obvious; breaking up with anyone is very difficult thing to do. Have you ever had to break up with someone for a particular reason? Have you ever had very messy break up you wish you could have handled better? I've heard many people say if they could go back and change something about their past relationships, they would have changed their own perspectives. I would agree taking a self-evaluation test is a very difficult thing to do. The truth is most people refuse to take blame for the failure of their relationships. It's a proven fact; most people take the easy road when it comes to actually exploring true love. As we know "love" is a very scary emotion which causes many people to take off running for the hills. I know this to be true, seeing how I use to be the first one to tell you love scared the hell of me. I was scared of love because I didn't want to lose anyone out of my life anymore. I reached a certain point in my life when I got tried of losing people who I considered dear to my heart. I recall sitting in the dark asking myself what did a normal life of love look like for me? Truthfully you'd be amazed how many times I failed to envision myself as a happy man. Sometimes we get so caught up in what we think we should have, we gradually over look what we do have. Love is a true reflection of self, and how the perception of others affects you. Here's a better way of looking at relationships if you care to entertain my embellishments. Love only creates three types of people in the animal kingdom of life. There's the prey, which despite many other disadvantages, usually becomes the brunt of every joke. The prey of love cries complains, and views complicated situations as the greatest mountain they can't climb. Many people would say cowards and prey resemble each another greatly. Now a predator is a totally different entity altogether as we've grown to witness from watching animal planet. I know when you hear the word **predator**, like many other people, it makes you feel a certain way. And you're completely right; a predator preys on the dispositions of others. The bold truth reflects everything we perceive to be true, and anyone who has ever been a victim of anything would tell you, at first you get bit by love then one day you start doing all the biting. Now the third kind of person in the life of love is greater than them both. The third kind of person is called a super predator, formally known as an apex predator. Without question you don't see many super predators of love anymore, there almost like an endangered species. The super predator of love sits in a category and rank of its own. By creating a diamond bond, you allow yourself to be measured by the likes of ambition, affection, and unbelievable desire for your significant other.

    What kind of animal are you in the scope of love?

    Are you prey, predator, or super predator?

A Guide To Understanding Your Mate, And Yourself A Little Bit Better

Inner Peace

It's evident; to be truly happy in life inner peace must play a very vital role. The soul of every being searches for inner peace during its lifetime. Every being tries to find what settles the soul and rejuvenates purpose of life. For some it may be food, religion, reading, writing, sports, music, cleaning, cooking, family, drawing, painting, building, and some even believe their purpose is destroying things in life. Most people sit back and marvel at their inner peace with a sense of achievement warming their hearts. A deep sigh sweeps over them at that moment, knowing they are truly satisfied where they are at in their lives. I always say each piece I write is like a favorite child, and I know were not to say we have a favorite child but we all do. You might have to explore the feelings within your heart and discover your passion to find this inner peace. Just remember your inner peace won't always be found on the surface, but everything derives from somewhere. The moment you find that place of peace in your heart you'll know exactly what it means to you. When you discover this state of inner peace you won't be able to think of nothing else or do anything else outside of what brings you this peace. You'll look up one day and silently say to yourself "I am what I've always dreamed I would be." Be warned though, it takes a certain type of person to be able to deal with all the elements which comes with attaining an inner peace. What I mean by it takes a certain type of person to be able to deal with what comes with attaining an inner peace is you have to reach a state of comfort in your heart. Your entire essence will be transformed beyond your comprehension when you discover your state of inner peace. And the sad truth is everyone won't understand this new profound state of peace inside your heart, which will cause them to try to rattle you or disturb this inner peace within you. The courage to be who you really are in the mist of your new profound liberation will free your soul, and enhance your current bond with significant other. Here's a short passage I begged Maykayla to share with the world, seeing how I thought it painted a very profound perspective on inner peace.

Us over All

We're all alone
At last a rose meets a thorn
Born into two different worlds of falsehood
Trying to discover something good
Only if we could
Only if mothers and fathers did what they should
It would be a perfect world wouldn't you agree
But it's not
So just like me
We look about to see
Innocent hearts striving to be free
Young souls become old souls on our journeys
Tortured for their purpose to called one another family
But sometimes family isn't what we paint in the mirror
Sometimes it's like dancing in the rain
It's like I prayed for you
Even in the mist of all my pain

A Guide To Understanding Your Mate, And Yourself A Little Bit Better

> Even when I felt like I had nothing to gain
> Like a house fire, I ask what remains.
> Trading ashes for memories
> Us over all

Terminus

With our journey coming to an end we only hope something shared in this passage gave you a sense of solace or greater understanding. The main message we wanted the lovers of the world to take away from this book was perfect bonds don't exist, we know that but there is a such thing as striving for something together. Maykayla has a great quote she always says "we are the same person in separate bodies sharing one heart." This means you and your significant other have to be willing to create a bond which can stand the test of time. It's no mystery to discover everyone believes in their state of love when it hasn't faced the likes of any fire, but the true test is when you're bond takes a couple of heavy hits and overcomes them. One of the main things we must never forget is love does not reward punks. Love doesn't know how to honor weakness, this is forever true. If you are someone who understands how love actually operates then you are very much ahead of everyone else. If you and your significant other aren't afraid to struggle to get to where you want or feel comfortable, you will be just fine in life. But the sad truth is if you are a coward or someone who avoids the hard lessons in life that love is always willing to give us, you will never know the sweet reward of caring for another soul. You have to be willing to be truly fearless when you love anything, especially one of universe's beautiful creatures. We both thank you and salute you all for growing with love and challenging yourselves to achieve a higher sense of art called the diamond bond.

    Maykayla Scott is an activist of women's rights and human empowerment. She finds peace in speaking with others, and sharing her story with many people all over the state of Colorado and the entire world. Since the release of this book Maykayla has earned her freedom and strives to help William S. Graham regain his freedom as well. Maykayla and William are closer than ever, keeping the faith of God at the helm of their lives. Maykayla and William are putting their focus on the future with true guidance from their family pastor/mentor Dr. John Dee Jeffries, who made this opportunity possible. Just know William S. Graham has shifted his focus toward helping others to fulfill their writing dreams as well as empowering them through hope, love, and understanding. Look forward to seeing a lot more from them in the near future to come.

    Thank you

A Diamond Bond is a relationship guide manual which encourages the lovers of the world to ask themselves one simple question, what kind of bond do I have with my significant other? It's true once you've read one relationship based book; you've read them all right! Not in this case I would say, seeing how this book is written by individuals who have seen the insides of a state penitentiary. A Diamond Bond donates a bold in your face approach toward relationships and having faith in something greater than us all…love. (Latin) ne cede malis – yield not to misfortunes

May God bless us all who seek love, forgiveness, wisdom, patience, truth, and growth?

www.ingramcontent.com/pod-product-compliance
Lightning Source LLC
Chambersburg PA
CBHW052156110526
44591CB00012B/1973